GENOCIDE & PERSECUTION

Burma

Titles in the Genocide and Persecution Series

GENOCIDE & PERSECUTION

| Burma

Noah Berlatsky
Book Editor

Frank Chalk
Consulting Editor

GREENHAVEN PRESS
A part of Gale, Cengage Learning

GALE
CENGAGE Learning·

Farmington Hills, Mich • San Francisco • New York • Waterville, Maine
Meriden, Conn • Mason, Ohio • Chicago

Patricia Coryell, *Vice President & Publisher, New Products & GVRL*
Douglas Dentino, *Manager, New Products*
Judy Galens, *Acquisitions Editor*

For more information, contact:
Greenhaven Press
27500 Drake Rd.
Farmington Hills, MI 48331-3535
Or you can visit our Internet site at gale.cengage.com.

For product information and technology assistance, contact us at:

Gale Customer Support, 1-800-877-4253
For permission to use material from this text or product, submit all requests online at www.cengage.com/permissions

Further permissions questions can be emailed to permissionrequest@cengage.com

Every effort is made to ensure that Greenhaven Press accurately reflects the original intent of the authors. Every effort has been made to trace the owners of copyrighted material.

Cover image © Paula Bronstein/Getty Images.
Interior barbed wire artwork © f9photos, used under license from Shutterstock.com.

LIBRARY OF CONGRESS CATALOGING-IN-PUBLICATION DATA

Burma / Noah Berlatsky, book editor.
    pages cm -- (Genocide and persecution)
    Includes bibliographical references and index.
    ISBN 978-0-7377-7230-2 (hardcover)
    1. Rohingya (Burmese people)--Violence against. 2. Minorities--Burma--Crimes against. I. Berlatsky, Noah, editor. II. Series: Genocide and persecution.
    DS528.2.R64B87 2015
    364.15'109591--dc23

                                                          2014035340

Printed in the United States of America
1 2 3 4 5 6 7 19 18 17 16 15

Contents

An American news agency reports on the election of longtime democracy champion Aung San Suu Kyi to Burma's parliament. The event is an important milestone in the transition from the nation's military dictatorship.

Chapter 2: Controversies Surrounding the Rohingya in Burma

Preface

> "For the dead and the living, we must
> bear witness."
>
> Elie Wiesel, Nobel laureate and
> Holocaust survivor

The histories of many nations are shaped by horrific events involving torture, violent repression, and systematic mass killings. The inhumanity of such events is difficult to comprehend, yet understanding why such events take place, what impact they have on society, and how they may be prevented in the future is vitally important. The Genocide and Persecution series provides readers with anthologies of previously published materials on acts of genocide, crimes against humanity, and other instances of extreme persecution, with an emphasis on events taking place in the twentieth and twenty-first centuries. The series offers essential historical background on these significant events in modern world history, presents the issues and controversies surrounding the events, and provides first-person narratives from people whose lives were altered by the events. By providing primary sources, as well as analysis of crucial issues, these volumes help develop critical-thinking skills and support global connections. In addition, the series directly addresses curriculum standards focused on informational text and literary nonfiction and explicitly promotes literacy in history and social studies.

Each Genocide and Persecution volume focuses on genocide, crimes against humanity, or severe persecution. Material from a variety of primary and secondary sources presents a multinational perspective on the event. Articles are carefully edited and introduced to provide context for readers. The series includes volumes on significant and widely studied events like the Holocaust, as well as events that are less often studied, such as the East Pakistan genocide in what is now Bangladesh. Some volumes focus on multiple events endured by a specific people, such as the Kurds, or multiple events enacted over time by a particular oppressor or in a particular location, such as the People's Republic of China.

Each volume is organized into three chapters. The first chapter provides readers with general background information and uses primary sources such as testimony from tribunals or international courts, documents or speeches from world leaders, and legislative text. The second chapter presents multinational perspectives on issues and controversies and addresses current implications or long-lasting effects of the event. Viewpoints explore such topics as root causes; outside interventions, if any; the impact on the targeted group and the region; and the contentious issues that arose in the aftermath. The third chapter presents first-person narratives from affected people, including survivors, family members of victims, perpetrators, officials, aid workers, and other witnesses.

In addition, numerous features are included in each volume of Genocide and Persecution:

- An annotated **table of contents** provides a brief summary of each essay in the volume.

- A **foreword** gives important background information on the recognition, definition, and study of genocide in recent history and examines current efforts focused on the prevention of future atrocities.

- A **chronology** offers important dates leading up to, during, and following the event.

- **Primary sources**—including historical newspaper accounts, testimony, and personal narratives—are among the varied selections in the anthology.

- **Illustrations**—including a world map, photographs, charts, graphs, statistics, and tables—are closely tied to the text and chosen to help readers understand key points or concepts.

- **Sidebars**—including biographies of key figures and overviews of earlier or related historical events—offer additional content.
- **Pedagogical features**—including analytical exercises, writing prompts, and group activities—introduce each chapter and help reinforce the material. These features promote proficiency in writing, speaking, and listening skills and literacy in history and social studies.
- A **glossary** defines key terms, as needed.
- An annotated list of international **organizations to contact** presents sources of additional information on the volume topic.
- A **list of primary source documents** provides an annotated list of reports, treaties, resolutions, and judicial decisions related to the volume topic.
- A **for further research** section offers a bibliography of books, periodical articles, and Internet sources and an annotated section of other items such as films and websites.
- A comprehensive subject **index** provides access to key people, places, events, and subjects cited in the text.

The Genocide and Persecution series illuminates atrocities that cannot and should not be forgotten. By delving deeply into these events from a variety of perspectives, students and other readers are provided with the information they need to think critically about the past and its implications for the future.

Foreword

The term *genocide* often appears in news stories and other literature. It is not widely known, however, that the core meaning of the term comes from a legal definition, and the concept became part of international criminal law only in 1951 when the United Nations Convention on the Prevention and Punishment of the Crime of Genocide came into force. The word *genocide* appeared in print for the first time in 1944 when Raphael Lemkin, a Polish Jewish refugee from Adolf Hitler's World War II invasion of Eastern Europe, invented the term and explored its meaning in his pioneering book *Axis Rule in Occupied Europe*.

Humanity's Recognition of Genocide and Persecution

Lemkin understood that throughout the history of the human race there have always been leaders who thought they could solve their problems not only through victory in war, but also by destroying entire national, ethnic, racial, or religious groups. Such annihilations of entire groups, in Lemkin's view, deprive the world of the very cultural diversity and richness in languages, traditions, values, and practices that distinguish the human race from all other life on earth. Genocide is not only unjust, it threatens the very existence and progress of human civilization, in Lemkin's eyes.

Looking to the past, Lemkin understood that the prevailing coarseness and brutality of earlier human societies and the lower value placed on human life obscured the existence of genocide. Sacrifice and exploitation, as well as torture and public execution, had been common at different times in history. Looking toward a more humane future, Lemkin asserted the need to punish— and when possible prevent—a crime for which there had been no name until he invented it.

Legal Definitions of Genocide

On December 9, 1948, the United Nations adopted its Convention on the Prevention and Punishment of the Crime of Genocide (UNGC). Under Article II, genocide

> means any of the following acts committed with intent to destroy, in whole or in part, a national, ethnical, racial or religious group, as such:
>
> (a) Killing members of the group;
>
> (b) Causing serious bodily or mental harm to members of the group;
>
> (c) Deliberately inflicting on the group conditions of life calculated to bring about its physical destruction in whole or in part;
>
> (d) Imposing measures intended to prevent births within the group;
>
> (e) Forcibly transferring children of the group to another group.

Article III of the convention defines the elements of the crime of genocide, making punishable:

> (a) Genocide;
>
> (b) Conspiracy to commit genocide;
>
> (c) Direct and public incitement to commit genocide;
>
> (d) Attempt to commit genocide;
>
> (e) Complicity in genocide.

After intense debate, the architects of the convention excluded acts committed with intent to destroy social, political, and economic groups from the definition of genocide. Thus, attempts to destroy whole social classes—the physically and mentally challenged, and homosexuals, for example—are not acts of genocide under the terms of the UNGC. These groups achieved a belated but very significant measure of protection under international criminal law in the Rome Statute of the International Criminal

Court, adopted at a conference on July 17, 1998, and entered into force on July 1, 2002.

The Rome Statute defined a crime against humanity in the following way:

> any of the following acts when committed as part of a widespread and systematic attack directed against any civilian population:
>
> (a) Murder;
>
> (b) Extermination;
>
> (c) Enslavement;
>
> (d) Deportation or forcible transfer of population;
>
> (e) Imprisonment or other severe deprivation of physical liberty in violation of fundamental rules of international law;
>
> (f) Torture;
>
> (g) Rape, sexual slavery, enforced prostitution, forced pregnancy, enforced sterilization, or any other form of sexual violence of comparable gravity;
>
> (h) Persecution against any identifiable group or collectivity on political, racial, national, ethnic, cultural, religious, gender . . . or other grounds that are universally recognized as impermissible under international law, in connection with any act referred to in this paragraph or any crime within the jurisdiction of this Court;
>
> (i) Enforced disappearance of persons;
>
> (j) The crime of apartheid;
>
> (k) Other inhumane acts of a similar character intentionally causing great suffering, or serious injury to body or to mental or physical health.

Although genocide is often ranked as "the crime of crimes," in practice prosecutors find it much easier to convict perpetrators of crimes against humanity rather than genocide under domestic laws. However, while Article I of the UNGC declares that countries adhering to the UNGC recognize genocide as "a crime under international law which they undertake to prevent and to punish," the Rome Statute provides no comparable international mechanism for the prosecution of crimes against humanity. A treaty would help individual countries and international institutions introduce measures to prevent crimes against humanity, as well as open more avenues to the domestic and international prosecution of war criminals.

The Evolving Laws of Genocide

In the aftermath of the serious crimes committed against civilians in the former Yugoslavia since 1991 and the Rwanda genocide of 1994, the United Nations Security Council created special international courts to bring the alleged perpetrators of these events to justice. While the UNGC stands as the standard definition of genocide in law, the new courts contributed significantly to today's nuanced meaning of genocide, crimes against humanity, ethnic cleansing, and serious war crimes in international criminal law.

Also helping to shape contemporary interpretations of such mass atrocity crimes are the special and mixed courts for Sierra Leone, Cambodia, Lebanon, and Iraq, which may be the last of their type in light of the creation of the International Criminal Court (ICC), with its broad jurisdiction over mass atrocity crimes in all countries that adhere to the Rome Statute of the ICC. The Yugoslavia and Rwanda tribunals have already clarified the law of genocide, ruling that rape can be prosecuted as a weapon in committing genocide, evidence of intent can be absent when convicting low-level perpetrators of genocide, and public incitement to commit genocide is a crime even if genocide does not immediately follow the incitement.

Several current controversies about genocide are worth noting and will require more research in the future:

1. Dictators accused of committing genocide or persecution may hold onto power more tightly for fear of becoming

vulnerable to prosecution after they step down. Therefore, do threats of international indictments of these alleged perpetrators actually delay transfers of power to more representative rulers, thereby causing needless suffering?

2. Would the large sum of money spent for international retributive justice be better spent on projects directly benefiting the survivors of genocide and persecution?

3. Can international courts render justice impartially or do they deliver only "victors' justice," that is the application of one set of rules to judge the vanquished and a different and laxer set of rules to judge the victors?

It is important to recognize that the law of genocide is constantly evolving, and scholars searching for the roots and early warning signs of genocide may prefer to use their own definitions of genocide in their work. While the UNGC stands as the standard definition of genocide in law, the debate over its interpretation and application will never end. The ultimate measure of the value of any definition of genocide is its utility for identifying the roots of genocide and preventing future genocides.

Motives for Genocide and Early Warning Signs

When identifying past cases of genocide, many scholars work with some version of the typology of motives published in 1990 by historian Frank Chalk and sociologist Kurt Jonassohn in their book *The History and Sociology of Genocide*. The authors identify the following four motives and acknowledge that they may overlap, or several lesser motives might also drive a perpetrator:

1. To eliminate a real or potential threat, as in Imperial Rome's decision to annihilate Carthage in 146 B.C.

2. To spread terror among real or potential enemies, as in Genghis Khan's destruction of city-states and people who rebelled against the Mongols in the thirteenth century.

3. To acquire economic wealth, as in the case of the Massachusetts Puritans' annihilation of the native Pequot people in 1637.
4. To implement a belief, theory, or an ideology, as in the case of Germany's decision under Hitler and the Nazis to destroy completely the Jewish people of Europe from 1941 to 1945.

Although these motives represent differing goals, they share common early warning signs of genocide. A good example of genocide in recent times that could have been prevented through close attention to early warning signs was the genocide of 1994 inflicted on the people labeled as "Tutsi" in Rwanda. Between 1959 and 1963, the predominantly Hutu political parties in power stigmatized all Tutsi as members of a hostile racial group, violently forcing their leaders and many civilians into exile in neighboring countries through a series of assassinations and massacres. Despite systematic exclusion of Tutsi from service in the military, government security agencies, and public service, as well as systematic discrimination against them in higher education, hundreds of thousands of Tutsi did remain behind in Rwanda. Government-issued cards identified each Rwandan as Hutu or Tutsi.

A generation later, some Tutsi raised in refugee camps in Uganda and elsewhere joined together, first organizing politically and then militarily, to reclaim a place in their homeland. When the predominantly Tutsi Rwanda Patriotic Front invaded Rwanda from Uganda in October 1990, extremist Hutu political parties demonized all of Rwanda's Tutsi as traitors, ratcheting up hate propaganda through radio broadcasts on government-run Radio Rwanda and privately owned radio station RTLM. Within the print media, *Kangura* and other publications used vicious cartoons to further demonize Tutsi and to stigmatize any Hutu who dared advocate bringing Tutsi into the government. Massacres of dozens and later hundreds of Tutsi sprang up even as Rwandans prepared to elect a coalition government led by moderate political parties, and as the United Nations dispatched a small international military force led by Canadian general Roméo Dallaire to oversee the elections and political transition. Late in 1992, an international human rights organization's investigating team detected the hate propaganda campaign, verified systematic massacres of Tutsi, and warned the international community that Rwanda had already entered the early stages of genocide, to no avail. On April 6, 1994, Rwanda's genocidal killing accelerated at an alarming pace when someone shot down the airplane flying Rwandan president Juvenal Habyarimana home from peace talks in Arusha, Tanzania.

Hundreds of thousands of Tutsi civilians—including children, women, and the elderly—died horrible deaths because the world ignored the early warning signs of the genocide and refused to act. Prominent among those early warning signs were: 1) systematic, government-decreed discrimination against the Tutsi as members of a supposed racial group; 2) government-issued identity cards labeling every Tutsi as a member of a racial group; 3) hate propaganda casting all Tutsi as subversives and traitors; 4) organized assassinations and massacres targeting Tutsi; and 5) indoctrination of militias and special military units to believe that all Tutsi posed a genocidal threat to the existence of Hutu and would enslave Hutu if they ever again became the rulers of Rwanda.

Genocide Prevention and the Responsibility to Protect

The shock waves emanating from the Rwanda genocide forced world leaders at least to acknowledge in principle that the national sovereignty of offending nations cannot trump the responsibility of those governments to prevent the infliction of mass atrocities on their own people. When governments violate that obligation, the member states of the United Nations have a responsibility to get involved. Such involvement can take the form of, first, offering to help the local government change its ways through technical advice and development aid, and second—if the local government persists in assaulting its own people—initiating armed intervention to protect the civilians at risk. In 2005 the United Nations began to implement the Responsibility to Protect initiative, a framework of principles to guide the international community in preventing mass atrocities.

As in many real-world domains, theory and practice often diverge. Genocide and crimes against humanity are rooted in problems that produce failing states: poverty, poor education, extreme nationalism, lawlessness, dictatorship, and corruption. Implementing the principles of the Responsibility to Protect doctrine burdens intervening state leaders with the necessity of addressing each of those problems over a long period of time. And when those problems prove too intractable and complex to solve easily, the citizens of the intervening nations may lose patience, voting out the leader who initiated the intervention. Arguments based solely on humanitarian principles fail to overcome such concerns. What is needed to persuade political leaders to stop preventable mass atrocities are compelling arguments based on their own national interests.

Preventable mass atrocities threaten the national interests of all states in five specific ways:

1. Mass atrocities create conditions that engender widespread and concrete threats from terrorism, piracy, and other forms of lawlessness on the land and sea;

2. Mass atrocities facilitate the spread of warlordism, whose tentacles block affordable access to vital raw materials produced in the affected country and threaten the prosperity of all nations that depend on the consumption of these resources;

3. Mass atrocities trigger cascades of refugees and internally displaced populations that, combined with climate change and growing international air travel, will accelerate the worldwide incidence of lethal infectious diseases;

4. Mass atrocities spawn single-interest parties and political agendas that drown out more diverse political discourse in the countries where the atrocities take place and in the countries that host large numbers of refugees. Xenophobia and nationalist backlashes are the predictable consequences of government indifference to mass atrocities elsewhere that could have been prevented through early actions;

5. Mass atrocities foster the spread of national and transnational criminal networks trafficking in drugs, women, arms, contraband, and laundered money.

Alerting elected political representatives to the consequences of mass atrocities should be part of every student movement's agenda in the twenty-first century. Adam Smith, the great political economist and author of *The Wealth of Nations*, put it best when he wrote: "It is not from the benevolence of the butcher, the brewer, or the baker that we expect our dinner, but from their regard to their own interest." Self-interest is a powerful engine for good in the marketplace and can be an equally powerful motive and source of inspiration for state action to prevent genocide and mass persecution. In today's new global village, the lives we save may be our own.

Frank Chalk

Frank Chalk, who has a doctorate from the University of Wisconsin–Madison, is a professor of history and director of the Montreal Institute for Genocide and Human Rights Studies at Concordia University in Montreal, Canada. He is coauthor, with Kurt Jonassohn, of The History and Sociology of Genocide *(1990); coauthor, with General Roméo Dallaire, Kyle Matthews, Carla Barqueiro, and Simon Doyle, of* Mobilizing the Will to Intervene: Leadership to Prevent Mass Atrocities *(2010); and associate editor of the three-volume Macmillan Reference USA* Encyclopedia of Genocide and Crimes Against Humanity *(2004). Chalk served as president of the International Association of Genocide Scholars from June 1999 to June 2001. His current research focuses on the use of radio and television broadcasting in the incitement and prevention of genocide, and domestic laws on genocide. For more information on genocide and examples of the experiences of people displaced by genocide and other human rights violations, interested readers can consult the websites of the Montreal Institute for Genocide and Human Rights Studies (http://migs.concordia.ca) and the Montreal Life Stories project (www.lifestoriesmontreal.ca).*

World Map

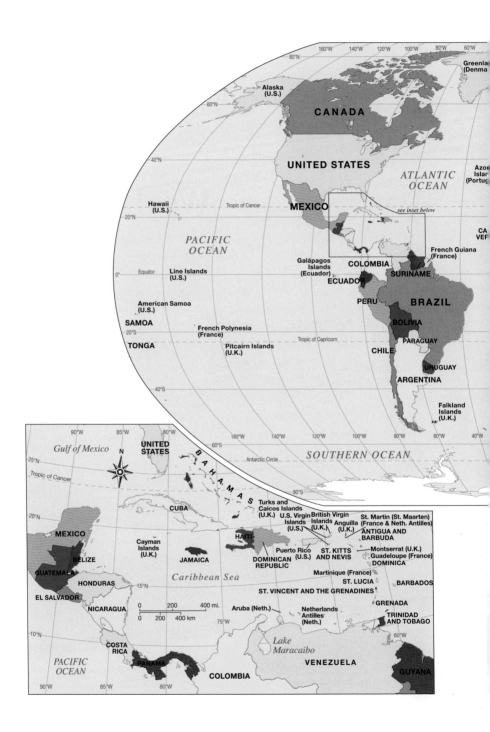

CANADA

UNITED STATES

ATLANTIC
OCEAN

Alaska
(U.S.)

Greenla
(Denma

Azo
Islar
(Portug

Hawaii
(U.S.)

Tropic of Cancer

MEXICO

see inset below

PACIFIC
OCEAN

Equator   Line Islands
(U.S.)

Galápagos
Islands
(Ecuador)

COLOMBIA

ECUADOR

SURINAME

French Guiana
(France)

CA
VEF

American Samoa
(U.S.)

SAMOA

French Polynesia
(France)

TONGA

Pitcairn Islands
(U.K.)

Tropic of Capricorn

PERU

CHILE

BOLIVIA

PARAGUAY

BRAZIL

URUGUAY

ARGENTINA

Falkland
Islands
(U.K.)

SOUTHERN OCEAN

Antarctic Circle

Gulf of Mexico   N

UNITED
STATES

BAHAMAS

Tropic of Cancer

MEXICO

CUBA

Cayman
Islands
(U.K.)

JAMAICA

HAITI

Turks and
Caicos Islands
(U.K.)   U.S. Virgin British Virgin
Islands   Islands   Anguilla
(U.S.)   (U.K.)   (U.K.)

Puerto Rico
(U.S.)

DOMINICAN
REPUBLIC

ST. KITTS
AND NEVIS

St. Martin (St. Maarten)
(France & Neth. Antilles)
ANTIGUA AND
BARBUDA

Montserrat (U.K.)
Guadeloupe (France)
DOMINICA

Martinique (France)

ST. LUCIA

ST. VINCENT AND THE GRENADINES

BARBADOS

GRENADA

TRINIDAD
AND TOBAGO

BELIZE

GUATEMALA

HONDURAS

EL SALVADOR

NICARAGUA

Caribbean Sea

0   200   400 mi.

0   200   400 km

Aruba (Neth.)

Netherlands
Antilles
(Neth.)

COSTA
RICA

PACIFIC
OCEAN

PANAMA

COLOMBIA

Lake
Maracaibo

VENEZUELA

GUYANA

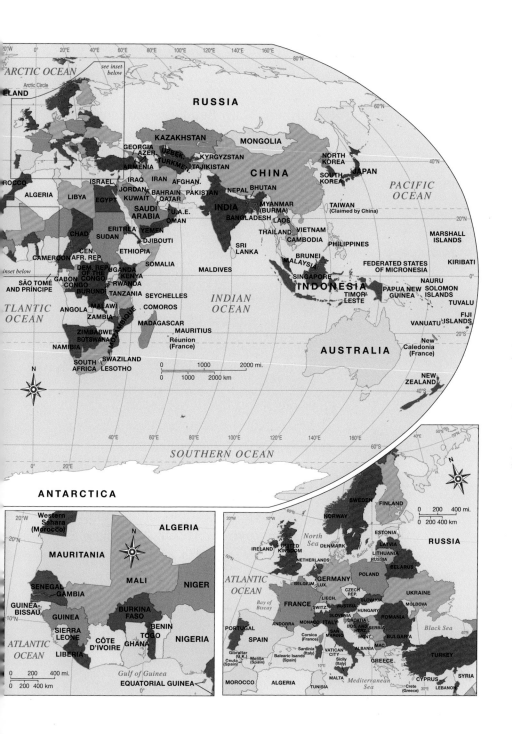

ARCTIC OCEAN

see inset
below

Arctic Circle

ELAND

RUSSIA

60°N

KAZAKHSTAN

MONGOLIA

GEORGIA
AZER.
ARMENIA
UZBEK.
TURKMEN.
KYRGYZSTAN
TAJIKISTAN

NORTH
KOREA

JAPAN

40°N

ROCCO

ISRAEL
IRAN
JORDAN
IRAQ
AFGHAN.
NEPAL
BHUTAN

CHINA

SOUTH
KOREA

PACIFIC
OCEAN

ALGERIA
LIBYA
EGYPT
KUWAIT
BAHRAIN
QATAR
PAKISTAN

SAUDI
ARABIA
U.A.E.
OMAN

INDIA

BANGLADESH

MYANMAR
(BURMA)
LAOS

TAIWAN
(Claimed by China)

20°N

CHAD
SUDAN
ERITREA
YEMEN
DJIBOUTI

THAILAND
VIETNAM
CAMBODIA

PHILIPPINES

MARSHALL
ISLANDS

CAMEROON
CEN.
AFR. REP.
ETHIOPIA

SRI
LANKA

BRUNEI
MALAYSIA

KIRIBATI

inset below

DEM. REP.
OF THE
CONGO
GABON
CONGO
UGANDA
KENYA
RWANDA
SOMALIA

MALDIVES

SINGAPORE

FEDERATED STATES
OF MICRONESIA

NAURU

0°

SÃO TOMÉ
AND PRÍNCIPE
BURUNDI
TANZANIA
SEYCHELLES

INDONESIA

TIMOR-
LESTE

PAPUA NEW
GUINEA

SOLOMON
ISLANDS

TLANTIC
OCEAN
ANGOLA
MALAWI
COMOROS

INDIAN
OCEAN

TUVALU

ZAMBIA
MOZAMBIQUE
MADAGASCAR

VANUATU
FIJI
ISLANDS

ZIMBABWE
BOTSWANA
MAURITIUS

20°S

NAMIBIA
SWAZILAND

Réunion
(France)

AUSTRALIA

New
Caledonia
(France)

SOUTH
AFRICA
LESOTHO

N

0   1000   2000 mi.

0   1000   2000 km

NEW
ZEALAND

40°S

40°E   60°E   80°E   100°E   120°E   140°E   160°E

60°S

SOUTHERN OCEAN

0°   20°E

ANTARCTICA

Western
Sahara
(Morocco)

ALGERIA

N

MAURITANIA

MALI

NIGER

SENEGAL
GAMBIA

GUINEA-
BISSAU
GUINEA
BURKINA
FASO
BENIN
TOGO

SIERRA
LEONE
CÔTE
D'IVOIRE
GHANA
NIGERIA

ATLANTIC
OCEAN
LIBERIA

Gulf of Guinea

0   200   400 mi.

0   200 400 km

EQUATORIAL GUINEA

SWEDEN
FINLAND

NORWAY

0   200   400 mi.

0   200 400 km

North
Sea
ESTONIA

IRELAND
UNITED
KINGDOM
DENMARK

Baltic Sea

LATVIA
LITHUANIA

RUSSIA

RUSSIA

NETHERLANDS

ATLANTIC
OCEAN

BELGIUM
LUX.
GERMANY

POLAND

BELARUS

Bay of
Biscay
FRANCE

LIECH.
SWITZ.
CZECH
REP.
AUSTRIA

SLOVAKIA

HUNGARY

UKRAINE

MOLDOVA

PORTUGAL
ANDORRA

SPAIN

MONACO
ITALY
SLOVENIA
CROATIA
BOS. AND
HERZ.
SAN
MARINO

ROMANIA

Black Sea

Corsica
(France)

Sardinia
(Italy)

MONT.

SERBIA

BULGARIA

Gibraltar
(U.K.)
Melilla
(Spain)
Ceuta
(Spain)
Balearic Isands
(Spain)

VATICAN
CITY
Sicily
(Italy)

ALBANIA
MAC.

GREECE

TURKEY

CYPRUS
SYRIA

MOROCCO
ALGERIA
TUNISIA

MALTA
Mediterranean
Sea
Crete
(Greece)

LEBANON

17

Chronology

1784	The Kingdom of Arakan falls to the Burmese. Many Buddhists and Muslims flee Arakan for Chittagong in current Bangladesh.
1823–1826	During the First Anglo-Burmese War, the British invade the Arakan province and conquer it.
1860–1875	Muslims and Buddhists who left Arakan to escape Burmese rule return from Chittagong.
1942	Japanese forces push the British out of Arakan during World War II. Fighting breaks out between Buddhists and Muslims. Many in the province flee to Chittagong. Most Buddhists end up in south Arakan; most Rohingya Muslims end up in the north. This division persists today.
1948	Burma's independent government is created. There is a civil war between the government and various ethnic groups. Muslims in north Arakan struggle for a Muslim state in north Arakan.
1960	Rohingya rights are recognized, and the Rohingya are able to vote in elections.
1962	Ne Win becomes Burma's head of state.
1978	General Ne Win directs "Operation Dragon King" against foreigners throughout Burma. The campaign is

particularly vicious in Rakhine (Arakan), where the Rohingya are targeted for execution and rape. As many as 250,000 Rohingya flee into Bangladesh.

1982   Ne Win's government passes a citizenship law, which gives full citizenship only to peoples of certain recognized races. This does not include Rohingya, who are effectively stripped of citizenship.

1988   Aung San Suu Kyi leads a democracy movement against military rule. Ne Win steps down, but the State Law and Order Restoration Council (SLORC) crushes the insurgency, reestablishes military rule, and kills thousands.

1990   SLORC allows elections in Rakhine, hoping the Rohingya will side with the government. They don't, and there are demonstrations throughout Burma.

1991   SLORC launches Operation Clean and Beautiful Nation, a new wave of repression. Another 250,000 Rohingya refugees move into Bangladesh, where they are housed in camps.

1992   Burma creates NaSaKa, an immigration police force that will be responsible for brutal, ongoing human rights violations against the Rohingya.

1994   NaSaKa places severe restrictions on Rohingya marriages. Most Rohingya have been repatriated from Bangladesh, but they still are not considered citizens by the Burmese government.

2007   Monks and demonstrators protest for democracy throughout Burma in a "Saffron Revolution." The military crushes the protests.

2008   Rohingya refugees attempt to escape by boat from Burma to Malaysia. The boats are stopped in Thailand; the Thai government decides to reject the refugees, pushing the boats out to sea without water or food. There is an international scandal when the boats are discovered after weeks with hundreds dead.

2010   Violence against the Rohingya continues and escalates. The first election in Burma in twenty years is held. The military party claims victory amidst charges of fraud. Aung San Suu Kyi is released from house arrest shortly after the election.

2011   Thein Sein becomes the nominally civilian president of Burma.

2012   Aung San Suu Kyi runs for Parliament and is elected. Violence between Buddhists and Muslims in Rohingya leaves many dead.

CHAPTER 1

Historical Background on the Rohingya in Burma

Chapter Exercises

STATISTICS	
	Burma
Total Area	676,578 sq km World ranking: 40
Population	55,746,253 World ranking: 25
Ethnic Groups	Burman 68%, Shan 9%, Karen 7%, Rakhine 4%, Chinese 3%, Indian 2%, Mon 2%, other 5%
Religions	Buddhist 89%, Christian 4% (Baptist 3%, Roman Catholic 1%), Muslim 4%, Animist 1%, other 2%
Literacy (total population)	92.7%
GDP	$111.1 billion World ranking: 71

Source: *The World Factbook*. Washington, DC: Central Intelligence Agency, 2014. www.cia.gov.

1. Analyzing Statistics

Question 1: What is the majority ethnic group in Burma? Approximately what percentage of the population are ethnic minorities?

Question 2: What is the majority religion in Burma? Approximately what percent of the population is Muslim?

Question 3: The source for the data in the chart comes from a source that includes 267 countries. Is Burma a relatively poor or rich country? Which statistic(s) did you use to make your determination?

2. Writing Prompt

Write an article about an attack on a Rohingya village. Give the story a strong title that will capture the audience's attention. Include background that would help your reader understand the reasons for the crisis. Give details that explain the overall crisis and answer who, what, when, where, and why.

3. Group Activity

Break into small groups and review Burma's 1982 Citizenship Law. Imagine your group is a new country. How would you define who is a citizen of your new nation? Consider what rights and privileges would be afforded by citizenship as well as potential issues of national security, economic development, daily life, and basic human rights. Discuss whether your country will have inclusive or exclusive citizenship policies. Then create a list of citizenship criteria for your new country. (Each list can be read aloud when the larger group reconvenes.)

History of the Persecution of the Rohingya

Kurt Jonassohn with Karin Solveig Björnson

The following viewpoint provides a historical overview of the plight of the Rohingya Muslims beginning with their origins in the Burmese state of Arakan in the ninth century. The authors report on centuries of brutal Burmese raids on the Arakan Rohingya and a history of conflicting interests and loyalties. The viewpoint indicates that this historical background set the stage for the humanitarian struggles and mass migrations that the Rohingya have had to face since the military took control of the Burmese government under General Ne Win in 1962. At the time of this writing, Kurt Jonassohn was a professor of sociology at Concordia University and director of the Montreal Institute for Genocide and Human Rights Studies, where his coauthor, Karin Solveig Björnson, was a research associate.

The Rohingyas live in Arakan state, sharing a border with Bangladesh and separated from Burma proper by the Arakan Yoma mountains. Between one and two million Rohingyas live in Arakan, making up more than half of the state's population. The Rohingyas are the descendants of foreign traders and soldiers, most notably Arab, Mongol, Turkish, Portuguese, and Bengali, who began to settle in Arakan after the ninth century, mixing with different native tribes. The Rohingyas converted to Islam in the fifteenth century when Arakan was a feudatory of Bengal. It was during this period that the Rohingyas developed their own distinct culture and art.

In the following centuries, Arakan was subjugated at various times by the armies of Burma and Portugal, leaving the area depopulated and impoverished. Burman raids on Arakan were frequent and brutal. In 1785 over 30,000 Burman soldiers attacked Arakan, destroying mosques, libraries, and cultural institutions. 20,000 prisoners were captured and brought back to Burma as slaves. Besides profiting materially from the plunder, the Burman monarchy saw these raids as a way of breaking the spirit of a people they considered foreign. Massacres of civilians were encouraged. During one of these raids, Rohingya men, women,

An aerial view shows the burned out Rohingya village of Myaebon in western Burma in 2012. Many Muslim villages have been completely destroyed during sectarian violence. © Soe Than Win/AFP/Getty Images.

and children were driven into bamboo enclosures and "burned alive by the hundreds."

British Rule and Its Aftermath

With the memory of Burma brutality fresh in their minds, the Rohingyas welcomed British rule in 1825, recognizing that they would be well-protected from further military invasion on the part of Burma. Moreover, under the British, the Rohingyas enjoyed a certain degree of political and cultural autonomy; by the 1930s the Rohingyas were actively campaigning for independence.

During World War II the Rohingyas remained loyal to the British, even when they retreated into India. They paid dearly for this choice: advancing Japanese and Burman armies tortured, raped, and massacred thousands of Rohingyas and over 22,000 refugees fled to India. After reconquering the region in 1945, the British rewarded the Rohingyas for their loyalty by setting up a civilian administration for the Rohingyas in Arakan. The dream of Rohingya autonomy was rather short-lived, however, as Arakan state was incorporated into Burma in the 1948 treaty granting Burma her independence from Britain.

Burman-Rohingya relations, which were not very friendly to begin with, deteriorated rapidly. In 1948 Muslims were barred from military service. Muslim civil servants and policemen were replaced by Burman government and military officials; Rohingya leaders were arbitrarily placed under arrest. Rohingya refugees who had remained in India after the war were not permitted to return to Burma. Considered by the government as illegal immigrants, their properties were seized and resettled by Burman nationals.

Diplomatic negotiations having failed, the Rohingyas took up arms. The rebels made rapid progress, and by 1949 they occupied northern Arakan, having expelled the Burmans who had settled there. Although the government did respond militarily, the Rohingyas, even in rebellion, retained their rights to elect representatives to parliament and to appeal in the courts. In 1961 the rebellion in Arakan state was subdued and the area was placed under the administration of a number of experienced army officers.

Human Rights Violations During Military Rule

General Ne Win's military takeover of the government in 1962 brought tighter military control to the area and also marked the beginning of a series of military operations designed to victimize Rohingya rebels and civilians. Being highly suspicious of non-Buddhists, Muslims were perfect targets for the new military regime. The Rohingya secessionist movement was met with brutal force on the part of the Burman military and Ne Win's troops were highly visible in Arakan state, particularly in the 1970s and 1980s.

In 1974, Rohingyas were denied the right to vote and jails in Akjab and Rangoon became places of detention for Rohingyas suddenly considered "illegal immigrants." After widespread unrest, the Burman government began its project "Naga Min" (Operation Dragon King). There were widespread reports of forced labor, torture, rapes, and mass killing in Arakan state as the Burman government set forth its plan to push the Rohingyas off its territory. Ne Win's government stated that the Rohingyas were not Burma's citizens (Burma had refused to give citizenship cards to Rohingyas after 1970) and asserted that the refugees leaving for Bangladesh were illegal immigrants. In 1979 Ne Win, despite his own mixed Burman-Chinese heritage stated:

> Today you can see that even people of pure blood are being disloyal to the race and country but are loyal to others. If people of pure blood act this way, we must carefully watch people of mixed blood. Some people are of pure blood, pure Burmese heritage and descendants of genuine citizens. Karin, Kachin and so forth, are of genuine pure blood. But we must consider whether these people are completely our race, our Burmese people.

Over 210,000 Rohingyas arrived in Bangladesh in 1978, but most were repatriated that same year after an agreement with Burma's government. Ne Win's government was apparently bowing to international pressure from the U.N. and the United States.

Oppression of the Rohingya did not stop in 1978, however. The Burman government became involved in a systematic campaign of genocide against the Rohingyas. Villages were destroyed, mass killings of civilians took place, including those of two hundred Rohingyas in prayer in a mosque, and children as young as seven were forcibly conscripted. Between 1991 and 1992, over 250,000 Rohingya fled to Bangladesh. Although Bangladesh has been hospitable to the Rohingyas, it is also one of the world's poorest countries. The area where these refugees were living is considered to be the most unsafe place in the world. This was the area where a cyclone hit in 1991, killing over 113,000 people. Voluntary and involuntary repatriation of the Rohingya began after Burma and Bangladesh signed a repatriation treaty in 1992. In November 1993, the Burman government agreed to permit the United Nations High Commission for Refugees (UMHCR) to assist and monitor returned refugees. However, the United States Committee for Refugees (USCR) has found that Bangladesh authorities coerced many Rohingya refugees into repatriating and that many of these refugees did not believe they could refuse to repatriate under the UNHCR program. By the end of 1995, fewer than 55,000 Rohingya refugees remained in Bangladesh. The USCR has indicated that the continuing reports about human rights abuses in Arakan, the small number of UNHCR workers, their reliance on interpreters provided by the Burman government, the lack of international NGO activity and the returnees being sent to hard-to-reach areas, make it very difficult for the UNHCR to guarantee the safety of Rohingya refugees returning to Burma.

The 1982 Citizenship Law Excludes the Rohingya

Government of Burma

The following viewpoint is excerpted from the Burma Citizenship Law. The law was passed by the Burmese government in 1982 and is the current basis for citizenship in the country. It sets up a stratified citizenship system based on heritage in which citizens must belong to an indigenous race, have a grandparent from an indigenous race, be born to a citizen, or have lived in British Burma prior to 1942. The law as written excludes all Rohingya—as well as members of certain other ethnicities—from Burmese citizenship.

3. Nationals such as the Kachin, Kayah, Karen, Chin, Burman, Mon, Rakhine or Shan [Burmese ethnic groups] and ethnic groups as have settled in any of the territories included within the State as their permanent home from a period anterior to 1185 B.E., 1823 A.D. are Burma citizens.

4. The Council of State may decide whether any ethnic group is national or not.

5. Every national and every person born of parents, both of whom are nationals, are citizens by birth.

Government of Burma, "Burma Citizenship Law," October 15, 1982. Courtesy of Burma Citizenship Law.

6. A person who is already a citizen on the date this Law comes into force is a citizen. Action, however shall be taken under section 18 for infringement of the provision of that section.

7. The following persons born in or outside the State are also citizens:

a. persons born of parents, both of whom are citizens;

b. persons born of parents, one of whom is a citizen and the other an associate citizen;

c. persons born of parents, one of whom and the other a naturalized citizen;

d. persons born of parents one of whom is
   i. a citizen; or
   ii. an associate citizen; or
   iii. a naturalized citizen;
   and the other is born of parents, both of whom are associate citizens;

e. persons born of parents, one of whom is
   i. a citizen; or
   ii. an associate citizen; or
   iii. a naturalized citizen;
   and the other is born of parents, both of whom are naturalized citizens;

f. persons born of parents one of whom is
   i. a citizen; or
   ii. an associate citizen; or
   iii. a naturalized citizen;
   and the other is born of parents, one of whom is an associate citizen and the other a naturalized citizen.

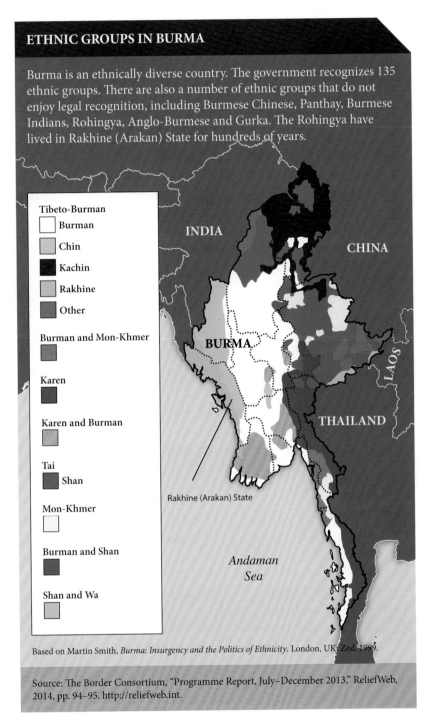

ETHNIC GROUPS IN BURMA

Burma is an ethnically diverse country. The government recognizes 135 ethnic groups. There are also a number of ethnic groups that do not enjoy legal recognition, including Burmese Chinese, Panthay, Burmese Indians, Rohingya, Anglo-Burmese and Gurka. The Rohingya have lived in Rakhine (Arakan) State for hundreds of years.

Tibeto-Burman
Burman
Chin
Kachin
Rakhine
Other

Burman and Mon-Khmer

Karen

Karen and Burman

Tai
Shan

Mon-Khmer

Burman and Shan

Shan and Wa

Rakhine (Arakan) State

INDIA

CHINA

BURMA

LAOS

THAILAND

Andaman
Sea

Based on Martin Smith, *Burma: Insurgency and the Politics of Ethnicity.* London, UK: Zed, 1999.

Source: The Border Consortium, "Programme Report, July–December 2013," ReliefWeb, 2014, pp. 94–95. http://reliefweb.int.

8. (a) The Council of State may, in the interest of the State, confer on any person citizenship or associate citizenship or naturalized citizenship.

(b) The Council of State may, in the interest of the State, revoke the citizenship or associate citizenship or naturalized citizenship of any person except a citizen by birth.

9. A person born in the State shall have his birth registered either by the parent or guardian in the prescribed manner, within [one] year from the date he completes the age of ten years, at the organizations prescribed by the Ministry of Home Affairs.

Proviso. If registration is not possible within one year from the date he completes the age of ten years, application may be made by the parent or guardian, furnishing sufficient reasons to the organizations prescribed by the Ministry of Home Affairs.

10. A person born outside the State shall have his birth registered either by the parent or guardian in the proscribed manner within one year from the date of birth at the Burmese Embassy or Consulate or organizations prescribed by the Ministry of Home Affairs.

Proviso. If registration is not possible within one year from the date of birth, application may be made by the parent or guardian, furnishing sufficient reasons to the Central Body through the Burmese Embassy or Consulate or organizations prescribed by the Ministry of Home Affairs.

11. (a) A parent or guardian who fails to comply with section 9 or section 10 shall be liable to pay a penalty of kyats fifty per year to the Burmese Embassy or Consulate or an organization prescribed by the Ministry of Home Affairs.

(b) A parent or guardian who fails for five years in succession to comply with section 9 or section 10 shall be liable to a penalty of kyats one thousand.

12. A citizen shall

a. respect and abide by the laws of the State;

b. discharge the duties prescribed by the laws of the State;

c. be entitled to enjoy the rights prescribed by the laws of the State.

13. A citizen shall not as well acquire the citizenship of another country.

14. A citizen shall have no right to divest himself of his citizenship during any war in which the State is engaged.

Rohingya Are Persecuted in the Early 1990s

Thomas K. Ragland

By the early 1990s, more than 220,000 Rohingya were living under harsh conditions in Bangladeshi refugee camps, according to the following viewpoint. The author maintains that these Rohingya refugees were escaping wanton cruelty at the hands of the Burmese military but found little relief in the provisional Bangladeshi camps. He goes on to describe efforts by the Bangladeshi government to repatriate refugees, even against their will, and outlines the United Nations' attempts to broker the repatriation process with an uncooperative Burmese government. Thomas K. Ragland is a founding partner of Benach Ragland LLP, an immigration attorney, and a former official in the US Department of Justice.

Since late 1991, large numbers of Muslims have fled their homes in Burma's northwestern Arakan state seeking refuge in neighboring Bangladesh. Striving to escape widespread murder, rape, torture, forced labor, and ethnic and religious persecution at the hands of the Burmese military, over 220,000 refugees, known as Rohingyas, now reside in makeshift camps along the border. Conditions in the camps have steadily worsened: as more refugees have arrived, the Bangladeshi government has withheld food rations, slowed the construction of shelter, and imposed other restrictive measures to compel the refugees to return to Burma. Many refugees have even been beaten, raped, and robbed by local police. In addition, the Rohingyas—particularly the children—suffer increasingly from a high death rate, a variety of health problems, and widespread malnutrition. Since December 1991 [through 1994], more than two thousand refugees have died in the camps.

In early 1992, the Burmese and Bangladeshi governments, with the involvement of the United Nations High Commissioner for Refugees (UNHCR), agreed on a plan to allow the return of some Muslims to Arakan. Enforcement of the agreement, however, immediately encountered difficulties. The UNHCR and the international community rejected Burma's terms, which not only limited reentry to those refugees who the government deemed "genuine citizens," but also did not guarantee that international groups would be allowed to monitor the repatriation process.

Fearful of further abuses by the Burmese military, refugees in the camps have vigorously resisted being returned to Arakan. Consequently, the repatriation process has slowed, although formal talks between the Burmese and Bangladeshi governments have continued. In the meantime, Bangladesh has tightened security in the camps, arrested or killed many who have protested the repatriation plan, compiled lists of refugees' names, and taken other steps to expedite the Rohingyas' departure. In November 1993, Burmese officials finally agreed to provide the UNHCR access to Rohingyas who are repatriated from Bangladesh and to allow international monitoring of the human rights situation in Arakan. Those refugees who return, however, face an uncertain future, including the risk of renewed abuses at the hands of the *tatmadaw*, Burma's 300,000-strong army. . . .

Restrictions on Rohingya Marriage

Since 1992, the regime has introduced a regulation that everyone in Northern Rakhine [Arakan] State is required to ask for prior permission of the authority before getting married. However, this restriction applies only to the Muslim population in this area, and not on the Buddhist Rakhine population, nor on any of the other smaller ethnic minority groups living in the region. Rohingyas and Muslims living in other parts of Myanmar are also not affected by this policy. However, prior permission itself may not be a problem, but what is problematic is that the authorities demand large amounts in taxes from people who ask for permission to get married. In some cases people have had to wait for two to three years to get permission, even after paying large sums of money, and they have had to go to the NaSaKa [the Burmese border security force] camp several times for it. According to the UDHR [Universal Declaration of Human Rights] (Article 16): 'men and women of full age, without any limitation due to race, nationality or religion, have the right to marry and to found a family.' The excessive and arbitrary fees and taxes imposed on Rohingya couples wishing to marry inhibits their ability to exercise this right. In general, most Rohingya couples must pay a substantial amount of money to the NaSaKa, varying from 50,000 to 300,000 kyat. Usually both the bride and groom each pay the same amount of money. Even after payment, sometimes permission is not given by the authority. This restriction especially affects poor people, who are unable to obtain such large amounts of money. Consequently, in some villages there have been no marriages at all since the late 1990s. There are also consistent reports of young couples fleeing to Bangladesh because this is the only way for them to get married. Once in Bangladesh it is very difficult for them to return, as their names have often been removed from their family list by the authorities.

Syed Serajul Islam, "State Terrorism in Arakan,"
A Handbook of Terrorism and Insurgency
in Southeast Asia, ed. Andrew T.H. Tan.
Northampton, MA: Edward Elgar, 2007, p. 338.

The Refugee Crisis of the Early 1990s

The situation in Arakan and along the Bangladeshi border today is strikingly similar to the situation that existed in 1978. Widespread religious persecution and the flagrant abuse of human rights has forced the current generation of Rohingyas to flee their homes and again seek protection in refugee camps on the opposite side of the Naaf River [the border with Bangladesh]. The outcome of the crisis has not yet been determined, however, and efforts should be made now to avoid a repeat of the disaster that occurred fifteen years ago.

In national elections on May 27, 1990, residents of Arakan (and other states throughout Burma) voted overwhelmingly in favor of opposition candidates, rejecting the military-backed National Unity Party. Following this widespread show of defiance, the army's campaign against ethnic minorities, which had intensified in 1989, grew into a "routine of concerted brutality" against the Rohingyas. By 1990, military forces effectively governed most of Arakan. The abuses most frequently perpetrated against Rohingyas by the Burmese army include forced labor and portering, rape, torture, religious persecution, confiscation of food supplies, and summary execution.

In interviews with human rights and humanitarian relief groups conducted in the refugee camps in Bangladesh, nearly all the Rohingya men reported having been repeatedly forced by soldiers to leave their homes, for days or weeks at a time, to work for the military. These interviews revealed that the Burmese army forces many Rohingyas to build roads, dig canals, or work on similar projects, while others must carry heavy loads of food, ammunition, and supplies. Porters also must often walk ahead of the troops to act as "human mine sweepers." Conditions are extremely harsh, as the soldiers provide little or no food and water, and beat those who work too slowly or fail to maintain pace. Laborers regularly die from starvation, fever, beatings, or exploding mines. The soldiers shoot and leave behind on the trail those who cannot work or fail to carry their burdens.

While the men are away, or often even when they are in the village, Burmese troops routinely and brutally rape Rohingya women and girls. The women must endure repeated rapes and beatings by a succession of soldiers, either in their homes or at military camps where the army often takes them in large groups. Many women die (usually by bleeding to death), whereas others are simply killed outright. Those who survive will likely be raped again.

Religious persecution against the Muslim Rohingyas has increased drastically since 1990. The Burmese army has locked up and destroyed mosques and Islamic schools (usually using forced Muslim laborers), beaten Rohingyas at prayer, prohibited most religious activity, and arrested and tortured teachers and students of Islam. Soldiers have seized Rohingya homes and moved non-Muslim Burmese into the appropriated houses. The army has even taken agricultural lands to use as housing project sites for newly arrived Buddhist residents.

The SLORC [Burma's military regime] began to insist, as previous officials had, that the Rohingyas were not Burmese citizens, but aliens who had crossed into the province illegally from Bangladesh. Identity cards issued to Muslims, without which they were forbidden to travel, designated them as "foreigners." In many cases, Burmese soldiers ordered Rohingyas to produce their identity cards and other citizenship materials, and then confiscated or destroyed the documents before their eyes. Numerous refugees have reported being told by the army that they were "Bangladeshis," and should "go home." The government campaign has been directed toward displacing the Muslims from their homes, taking their property, destroying their resistance, denying their proof of citizenship, and then forcing them out of the country. The sheer numbers of Rohingyas who have fled from Arakan attest to the success of the SLORC's policy.

In the Cox's Bazar district of Bangladesh, conditions in the fifteen camps that hold Rohingyas have steadily grown worse. When the refugees first began to arrive in 1990, the Bangladeshi government welcomed them, offered them support, and requested international cooperation to provide them with emergency assistance. As Rohingyas continued to arrive, however, sometimes by the thousands each day, officials attempted to reach an agreement with the SLORC that would provide for expedited repatriation. Faced with domestic pressures, limited resources, and scrutiny in the international media, Bangladesh's government became increasingly unwilling to care for the growing tide of refugees. Finally, in February 1992, Bangladeshi officials appealed to the international community for aid, and invited the UNHCR to assess the situation and to try to stop the influx of Rohingyas.

The UN Tries to Mediate

On March 24, 1992, U.N. Secretary-General Boutros Boutros Ghali issued a press release stating that the "tragic situation" in Burma, if not urgently addressed, would "threaten the stability of the region and increase human suffering. "In early April, Boutros-Ghali dispatched Ambassador Jan Eliasson, Under

Rohingya refugees wait to be returned to Burma from neighboring Bangladesh by the UN Refugee Agency (UNHCR) in 1997. © Dario Mitidieri/Edit by Getty Images.

Secretary-General for Humanitarian Affairs, to Bangladesh and Burma in an attempt to obtain a negotiated settlement of the refugee crisis. On April 28, 1992, with the assistance of Ambassador Eliasson, the Burmese foreign minister and his counterpart from Bangladesh signed an agreement providing for repatriation of the refugees. The plan called for the "safe and voluntary" return of 5,000 persons a day over a period of six months. Bangladesh offered to assist Burmese officials by registering Rohingyas in the camps and determining who among them carried "evidence of residence" in Burma. Burmese officials, however, agreed to admit only those individuals who could give "bona fide evidence of their residence in Myanmar" through official government documentation. The SLORC also refused to allow monitoring by the UNHCR of the refugees' safety once they were back inside Burma.

The UNHCR immediately withdrew its support for the agreement, and the international community demanded that repatriations not begin until U.N. observers could ensure the refugees' "safe and voluntary" return. Rohingyas inside the camps responded immediately by protesting the repatriation plan, but the demonstrations ended when Bangladeshi troops fired on a group of about 2,000 refugees, killing one and injuring twenty. The Burmese and Bangladeshi governments quickly suspended the planned repatriations indefinitely.

In the months that followed, Rohingyas in the camps continued to oppose Bangladesh's efforts to accelerate the repatriation process. Many refugees reportedly took up arms, and violent clashes between residents and government officials occurred inside several camps. At the same time, Bangladesh imposed further restrictive measures to suppress opposition and to encourage the Rohingyas to leave the country. In Burma, reports of atrocities in Arakan continued, and the SLORC repeated its unwillingness to allow UNHCR involvement in the repatriation process.

On September 22, 1992, Bangladesh began secretly returning Rohingyas to Arakan. Many Rohingyas reportedly refused to return to Burma unless the SLORC agreed to allow United Nations monitors to supervise the repatriation and resettlement process, and further conflicts between Bangladeshi police and residents of the camps ensued. The UNHCR announced on December 23, 1992 that Bangladesh had returned more than 4,000 persons to Burma, thereby violating the Bangladeshi authorities' pledge of "strict adherence to the principle of voluntary repatriation." In addition, the UNHCR stopped screening refugees because Bangladesh denied agency personnel free access to the camps to conduct confidential interviews.

On January 20, 1993, Bangladesh temporarily suspended repatriations and began negotiating with Sadako Ogata, U.N. High Commissioner for Refugees, to reestablish UNHCR participation in the repatriation proceedings. Prior to the hiatus, Bangladesh had returned more than 17,000 Rohingyas to Arakan, at least some of them involuntarily. Nine days later, Bangladeshi and UNHCR officials reached an agreement on renewed United Nations supervision of repatriation efforts, which resumed on February 1. Bangladesh's foreign minister declared that "[a]ll hindrances and misunderstandings on the refugee problems have been removed," and reaffirmed "the sincerity of Bangladesh and its firm policy toward voluntary repatriation." The UNHCR pledged full cooperation with the repatriation process. Burma's dictators, however, persistently refused to permit the UNHCR or any other group to monitor the repatriation and resettlement of Rohingyas in Arakan.

In May 1993, High Commissioner Ogata executed a formal Memorandum of Understanding with Bangladeshi officials, which included an agreement on the safe and voluntary return of Rohingyas to Burma, UNHCR access to the camps in Bangladesh, and international assistance to returnees. On November 5, 1993, a UNHCR representative signed a Memorandum of Understanding with the SLORC, guaranteeing the United Nations agency access to those refugees who return to Arakan. Although this agreement represents an important step in securing safe repatriation and resettlement for the refugees, the international community must maintain a vigilant watch over the SLORC's activities in Arakan. As historical events have illustrated, the Rohingyas are a target for abuse by the dictators in Rangoon [Burma's former capital].

The Rohingya Refugee Crisis of the 2000s

IRIN

The following viewpoint outlines several reasons why the Burmese refugee crisis in Southeast Asia has not improved in the 2000s. One reason the author gives is that the largest asylum countries —Thailand, Malaysia, Bangladesh, and India—have shown little interest in being anything other than provisional hosts. The author mentions that many of its neighbors consider Burma an important trading partner and would prefer not to compromise this relationship. Resettlement of refugees in a third country is the least ideal choice, according to the United Nations (UN) High Commissioner on Refugees, but may in this case be the only viable option. IRIN is a humanitarian news agency maintained by the UN.

A year ago [as of 2010], the world was shocked by images of boatloads of ethnic Rohingya refugees from Myanmar [Burma] being pushed out to open sea off the Thailand coast to fend for themselves with little food or water.

The plight of the Muslim Rohingya boat people from Myanmar's northern Rakhine [Arakan] State galvanized international attention, and highlighted a refugee crisis that seemingly has become part of the region's geopolitical make-up.

According to the UN Refugee Agency (UNHCR), Myanmar is the largest source of refugees in Southeast Asia; globally, it ranked 13th behind Iraq, Afghanistan and Somalia at end-2008.

In what is described by the UN and specialists as one of the world's most intractable refugee situations, people have been fleeing Myanmar for more than a quarter of a century.

Ethnic Conflicts Since the End of British Rule

Analysts say the root causes of Myanmar's refugee exodus lie in the ethnic and political conflicts since independence in 1948 from the British.

Myanmar, with an estimated population of 57.6 million, is one of the most ethnically diverse countries in Southeast Asia.

About two-thirds of the population are ethnic Burmese, while the remainder are Shan, Karen, Rakhine, Chinese, Mon and Indian, as well as the Akha, Chin, Danu, Kachin, Kokang, Lahu, Naga, Palaung, Pao, Rohingya, Tavoyan and Wa peoples. There are about 135 ethnic sub-groups, according to the government.

The minorities live mostly in the hills and mountains bordering Bangladesh, China, India, Laos and Thailand, while the Burmese are found in the central alluvial plains and major towns and cities.

The military, which has ruled Myanmar since 1962, has sought a centralized, unitary state, while ethnic groups want a federal structure and greater independence and autonomy, as well as greater recognition of their cultures.

"The root problem is that the government does not recognize ethnic aspirations and appears to want total military victory. Nothing will improve if that's what they want to do," said Jack Dunford, executive director of the Thailand Burma Border Consortium (TBBC), which provides food and shelter in nine refugee camps in Thailand [and is] one of 18 NGOs working in the camps.

While several armed ethnic groups have signed ceasefire agreements with the government, there are long-running insurgencies in the country's border regions by groups such as the Karen National Union (KNU).

The insurgencies, the government's counter-insurgency strategies and growing militarization have seen civilian populations increasingly bearing the brunt of the conflict and fleeing.

Forced labour by the military, the forced relocation of villages, enforced disappearances, rape and other forms of sexual violence, torture, arbitrary detentions, and discrimination against ethnic minorities are all cited as concerns in Myanmar by the UN and international rights groups.

Regional Action Urged to Help the Rohingya

Burmese refugee populations are mainly found in Thailand, Malaysia, Bangladesh and India, though some Rohingya travel as far afield as Saudi Arabia.

The refugees are vulnerable to human traffickers and people smugglers. Where there are no refugee camps, they receive little support and are routinely subject to detention, discrimination, harassment and exploitative working conditions, rights groups say.

None of the main asylum countries in Asia is a signatory to the 1951 Convention Relating to the Status of Refugees or its 1967 Protocol, leaving Burmese refugees with little protection or recognition of their rights.

Kitty McKinsey, regional spokeswoman for UNHCR, said many Asian countries lacked national refugee legislation, with the result that legitimate asylum seekers and refugees are instead treated as migrants in breach of immigration laws.

Countries "feel the right place for them is in an immigration detention centre. So they quite often put people in detention who we think are asylum seekers and refugees," she said.

With few prospects for change in Myanmar's domestic politics, rights groups have long urged regional governments to exert political pressure on the military government to reform.

"Burma has been like a pressure cooker and the international community has worked [hard] over the past few decades to ease the pressure minimally," said Debbie Stothard, coordinator of the rights group, ALTSEAN-Burma. "There hasn't been the political will to fundamentally resolve the root causes that have pushed people out of Burma."

The Association of Southeast Asian Nations [ASEAN], which includes Myanmar, has maintained a policy of "constructive engagement" with the country and does brisk trade with it.

Myanmar, rich in natural resources such as oil, gas, and timber, also counts regional superpowers China and India among its allies, helping to buffer international criticism.

"We need to understand holistically that all of these things are connected, that working with the regime for short-term gain or trying to accommodate the regime's misbehaviour for the sake of geopolitical interests entails the cost of receiving asylum seekers and hosting them," said Stothard.

Little Concrete Progress

Following the incident with the Rohingya boat people last year, ASEAN in March 2009 informally discussed the problem of Rohingya refugees, but found no solution. There were then hopes that a regional conference known as the Bali Process, which largely tackles human trafficking and people smuggling, could address the issue.

"For us it's an achievement that it even got on the agenda because we've been trying to get it on to the international and Asian agenda for years," said UNHCR's McKinsey.

At the Bali conference in April 2009, there was agreement on setting up an ad-hoc working group on the issue. However, little has been made public since about Bali Process discussions, or whether concrete actions will arise from this move.

"Though there are occasional flare-ups in relations, as was the case in the first months of 2009 over Rohingya boat people, these issues have been resolved more by pushing them back under the table than by providing real solutions that could benefit the refugee population," said Camilla Olson, an advocate for the US-based Refugees International.

"After 20 years, regional governments should acknowledge that a policy that ignores Burmese refugees will not make them go away," she said.

"Instead, it has created a new class of largely urban poor, who have few opportunities for education, healthcare, or productive futures."

Donor Fatigue

The intractable nature of the emergency is vividly illustrated by nine refugee camps in Thailand along the 1,800 km [118 mi] border with Myanmar, where some 150,000 Burmese live. Uniquely, the camps are run by the refugees themselves, with support from NGOs.

Rohingya refugees arrive on dry land after being rescued by fishermen in 2009 off the coast of Banda Aceh, Indonesia. The 193 men said that they were mistreated by Thai soldiers, then towed to sea and left to drift with inadequate supplies © AP Photo/Taufik Kurahman.

The genesis of these camps dates back to 1984, when the military government's bid to seize more control of areas in the east sent the first large influx of 10,000 mainly Karen refugees into Thailand.

The camps still exist, and with little end in sight to the flow of refugees, aid workers say the needs are greater than ever.

"We have had new refugees arriving every day for the last 25 years," said TBBC's Dunford. "We are dealing with an ongoing emergency, not something static."

Dunford said there was donor fatigue after so long, and few prospects that refugees could lead a normal life. Since anyone who ventures outside the camp is considered an illegal migrant, the ability of refugees to pursue productive lives and greater self-reliance by seeking employment or other activities is limited.

"As we go into 2010, our budgets are going up, the numbers [of refugees] are going up and we have this pressure now from donors wanting to see change," he said.

"We also want to see change, and in particular for the refugees to be more self-reliant. But change will take time, particularly when the Royal Thai Government is concerned about creating a pull factor by improving refugees' quality of life."

Dunford said that in the short term, additional funds were needed to support livelihood initiatives before basic support could be reduced.

Resettlement as a Final Viable Option

There are three solutions to any refugee crisis, says UNHCR: voluntary repatriation to the country of origin, integration into the asylum country, and resettlement in a third country as a final measure.

Recognizing that voluntary repatriation is not a real option, and that settling in asylum countries such as Thailand is difficult, donor countries have offered in recent years to resettle thousands of Burmese refugees.

Since 2004, the International Organization for Migration (IOM) has helped to resettle more than 57,000 Burmese refugees from Thailand who belonged to the Karen and Karenni ethnic groups. They were mostly resettled in the US, as well as Australia, Canada and New Zealand.

Michiko Ito, assistant resettlement coordinator with IOM in Bangkok, said countries would continue to be interested in resettling Burmese refugees, but that there was a shift away from accepting refugees out of Thailand, which had "peaked".

"The number out of Malaysia will definitely go up. And the resettlement countries are also looking into the resettlement of Rohingyas out of Bangladesh," said Ito.

Thailand has peaked because resettlement countries look at refugees' living conditions, and the camps provide better help than in Malaysia or Bangladesh, where refugee populations have little assistance, she said.

"In Malaysia, they are living in urban settings and there is absolutely no protection mechanism available for them," said Ito.

Opposition Party Says Burma's Suu Kyi Wins Parliament Seat

Associated Press

The following viewpoint outlines the significance of opposition leader Aung San Suu Kyi's 2012 election victory, which won her a seat in the Burmese parliament. The authors describe the elated public reaction in Burma to news of her victory. They also caution that her party's power to effect change will be limited since politicians from the previous regime still hold a majority of parliamentary seats. Even so, Suu Kyi's election represents a significant step toward national reconciliation and realignment with the international community, the viewpoint asserts. The Associated Press is an independent news service headquartered in New York.

Supporters of Burma's opposition icon Aung San Suu Kyi erupted in euphoric cheers Sunday [April 1, 2012] after her party said she won a parliamentary seat in a landmark election, setting the stage for her to take public office for the first time.

The victory, if confirmed, would mark a major milestone in the Southeast Asian nation, also called Myanmar, where the military has ruled almost exclusively for a half-century and where

National League for Democracy supporters celebrate the victory of Aung San Suu Kyi in Burma's parliamentary election in April 2012. © Paula Bronstein/Getty Images.

a new reform-minded government is seeking legitimacy and a lifting of Western sanctions.

It would also mark the biggest prize of Suu Kyi's political career, and a spectacular reversal of fortune for the 66-year-old Nobel Peace Prize laureate who the former junta had kept imprisoned in her lakeside home for the better part of two decades.

A Widely Celebrated Victory

The victory claim was displayed on a digital signboard outside the opposition National League for Democracy's [NLD] head-quarters in Burma's main city, Rangoon, where supporters gathered by the thousands as the polls closed in the late afternoon. They began wildly shouting upon learning the news, chanting "We won! We won!" while clapping, dancing, waving red party flags and gesturing with thumbs-up and V-for-victory signs.

As more counts came in from the NLD's poll watchers around the country, the crowd grew to as many as 10,000. The party's security guards tried without success to keep the traffic flowing past the people occupying much of the road and all nearby sidewalks.

By 9 P.M., the NLD was claiming victory in 13 constituencies, including two in the capital, Naypyitaw. It claimed substantial leads in about 10 more. No official tallies had been released.

Results in Naypyitaw had been hard to predict, because many of its residents are civil servants and their families dependent on the government for their livelihoods, and the turnout when Suu Kyi campaigned there was noticeably smaller than elsewhere. But the party appeared to be running up large leads over its rival, the ruling Union Solidarity and Development Party.

"It is the people's victory! We have taught them a lesson," said a shopkeeper who goes by the single name Thein who wore a T-shirt with Suu Kyi's picture on the front and her party's fighting peacock on the back.

The digital screen displaying results also flashed a message from Suu Kyi to her followers noting that they were understandably happy but should avoid gloating. She cautioned them to "Please refrain from rude behavior or actions that would make the other side unhappy."

Results were expected to come in slowly from more rural and remote areas. All results must be confirmed by the official electoral commission, however, which may not make an official declaration for days.

Suu Kyi's results were among the first announced; shortly after polls closed, her party had claimed that Suu Kyi was ahead with 65% of the vote in 82 of her constituency's 129 polling stations. The party had staff and volunteers spread throughout the vast rice-farming district, who were calling in preliminary results by phone to their headquarters in Rangoon.

The victory claim came despite allegations by her National League for Democracy party that "rampant irregularities" had taken place on voting day. Party spokesman Nyan Win said that by midday alone the party had filed more than 50 complaints to the Election Commission.

He said most alleged violations concerned waxed ballot papers that made it difficult to mark votes. There were also ballot cards that lacked the Election Commission's seal, which would render them invalid.

Sunday's by-election was called to fill just 45 vacant seats in Burma's 664-seat national Parliament and will not change the balance of power in a new government that is nominally civilian but still heavily controlled by retired generals. Suu Kyi and other opposition candidates would have almost no say even if they win all the seats they are contesting.

Suu Kyi's Symbolic and Strategic Role

But her candidacy has resurrected hope among Burma's downtrodden masses, who have grown up for generations under strict military rule. If Suu Kyi takes office as expected, it would symbolize a giant leap toward national reconciliation.

"She may not be able to do anything at this stage," said one voter, Go Khehtay, who cast his ballot for Suu Kyi at Wah Thin Kha, one of the dirt-poor villages in the rural constituency south of Rangoon that she is vying to represent. "But one day, I believe she'll be able to bring real change."

Earlier, crowds of supporters mobbed Suu Kyi as she visited a polling station in the village after spending the night there. The tiny community of 3,000 farmers has no electricity or running water, and its near-total underdevelopment illustrates the profound challenges facing the country as it slowly emerges from 49 years of army rule.

Despite the reports of widespread irregularities, a confirmed victory by Suu Kyi could cheer Western powers and nudge them closer to easing economic sanctions they have imposed on the country for years.

Suu Kyi herself told reporters Friday that the campaigning for Sunday's vote [had] been anything but free or fair, but that she was pressing forward with her candidacy because it's "what our people want."

Last year, Burma's long-entrenched military junta handed power to a civilian government dominated by retired officers that skeptics decried as a proxy for continued military rule. But the new rulers—who came to power in a 2010 vote that critics say was neither free nor fair—have surprised the world with a wave of reform.

The government of President Thein Sein, himself a retired lieutenant general, has freed political prisoners, signed truces with rebel groups and opened a direct dialogue with Suu Kyi, who wields enough moral authority to greatly influence the Burma policy of the U.S. and other powers.

Suu Kyi's decision to endorse Thein Sein's reforms so far and run in Sunday's election represents a political gamble.

Once in parliament, she can seek to influence policy and challenge the government from within. But she also risks legitimizing a regime she has fought against for decades while gaining little true legislative power.

Suu Kyi is in a "strategic symbiosis" with some of the country's generals and ex-generals, said Maung Zarni, a Burma expert and a visiting fellow at the London School of Economics.

"They need her and she needs them to break the 25 years of political stalemate," Zarni said. "She holds the key for the regime's need for its international acceptance and normalization."

Sunday's poll marks the first foray into electoral politics by Suu Kyi's National League for Democracy party since winning a landslide election victory in 1990. The military annulled those results and kept Suu Kyi in detention for much of the next two decades. The party boycotted the last vote in 2010, but in January the government amended key electoral laws, paving the way for a run in this weekend's ballot.

A new reform was expected Monday when Burma's currency will be largely unshackled from government controls that kept the kyat at an artificially high rate for decades. The International Monetary Fund says the change could lift a major constraint on growth in one of Asia's least developed countries.

Buddhists Attack the Rohingya in 2012

Mark Magnier

The following viewpoint describes an October 2012 flare-up of violence in the Burmese state of Arakan, also called Rakhine. The author acknowledges that the incident was the worst reported since earlier that year, but emphasizes that the violence is part of a continuing pattern in Arakan. Drawing parallels to the tensions in the Balkans following the collapse of the Soviet Union, he points out that ethnic strife and insurgencies are commonplace in other regions of Burma as well. The Burmese government has officially condemned the violence, according to the author, but its navy has impeded the safe passage of Rohingya refugees. Mark Magnier is a Wall Street Journal *correspondent covering economic issues in China and Taiwan.*

At least 112 people have been killed and thousands of houses burned as ethnic and religious violence in western Myanmar intensifies, according to news reports and community activists, as the government struggled to restore order, imposing dusk-to-dawn curfews in some areas and stepping up security.

Deadly violence between Buddhist ethnic Rakhine and Rohingya Muslims reportedly has spread to at least four townships
over recent days [as of October 26, 2012], although it's not clear
what sparked it. The most recent round of tit-for-tat attacks started
Sunday, but distrust between the communities goes back decades.

Growing Ethnic Violence in Rakhine State

On Thursday, [US] State Department spokeswoman Victoria Nu-
land urged the government of Myanmar, also known as Burma,
to try to immediately halt the violence as she called for unfettered
access to the affected area by international humanitarian groups.

Western Rakhine state, where the violence has occurred, is
grabbing the headlines, but Myanmar faces ethnic and religious
tension on several fronts. Although the recently installed civilian government has signed cease-fire agreements with several of
the country's ethnic groups, these don't amount to peace deals,
even as government troops continue to battle ethnic Kachin insurgents along the northern border with China.

Some have compared the current situation to sectarian
violence seen after the Soviet Union's collapse as ironclad rule
ended, leading to the airing of long-suppressed animosities. A
protracted war in the Balkans followed.

Those in Myanmar hope bloodshed can be contained even
as they acknowledge the risk. "The situation remains tense and
will remain so for the foreseeable future," said Aung Naing Oo,
member of a 27-person commission formed by the government
to investigate the violence, who returned from a weeklong trip to
Rakhine state Wednesday. "What I have seen or heard reminds
me of former Yugoslavia."

Aung said he saw smoke over Kyaukpyu township from
the air during this week's visits to Rakhine Buddhist and Muslim refugee camps. "Both the Rakhine and Muslims are victims
of neglect from the previous governments," he added. "As with
any conflict where blood is spilled, reconciliations are always
difficult."

On Thursday evening, some 50 Buddhist monks protested in front of Yangon's [Burma's largest city] Sule Pagoda, holding posters of Buddhists allegedly injured by Muslims. Popular opinion in Myanmar, including among Buddhist monks, is weighted against the Rohingya. One well-known monk, U Pyinar Thiha, said that if the government gives in to the Muslims, he'll leave the monkhood and join the army.

This week's flare-up involving the two communities is reportedly the worst since June, when over 80 Muslims and Buddhists were killed after an alleged rape, forcing at least 75,000 people from their homes. Many are still in makeshift camps.

Myanmar's increasingly open media has often been ahead of the government in reporting the conflict. Rakhine State Update News, a private website, said Friday the army opened fire on a boat carrying Rakhine Buddhists in Kyout Taw township on the Kalatan River, killing two and wounding 10. The report could not be confirmed. Rakhine Straight Views, another website, reported that arson attacks by both sides continued Friday.

Lawmaker Mann Maung Maung Nyan called on the central government Friday in parliament to increase security immediately and prevent human rights violations. The Home Affairs Ministry pledged to act swiftly against anyone breaking the law.

Violence this week has reportedly spread to Kyaukpyu, a commercial center that marks the start of a multibillion-dollar energy pipeline linking China and Myanmar.

Rakhine state spokesperson Win Myaing told Reuters on Friday that the death toll had reached 112. This followed a statement Thursday from the president's office placing the number of dead at 12, with 1,948 houses and eight religious buildings burned or otherwise destroyed.

"This violence will damage the dignity and interests of Myanmar's citizens," the presidential statement said. "We have also discovered that there are organizations and persons behind the agitations and will take legal action against them," it added, without providing details on the identity of alleged agitators.

Anti-Rohingya Prejudice

Immediately after the first wave of sectarian violence in June 2012, local Buddhist monks circulated pamphlets calling for the isolation of Muslims. For instance, on June 29, monks in Sittwe distributed an incendiary pamphlet to the local Arakanese population, telling all Arakanese that they "Must not do business with Bengalis [Rohingya]," and "Must not associate with Bengalis [Rohingya]." The pamphlet alleged that the Rohingya sought to eliminate the Arakanese population, stating that the "Bengalis [Rohingya] who dwell on Arakanese land, drink Arakanese water, and rest under Arakanese shadows are now working for the extinction of the Arakanese." It implored the people to follow the demands to socially and economically isolate the Rohingya to prevent the "extinction of the Arakanese."

The day the pamphlet was distributed, a Buddhist monk in Sittwe who spearheaded the effort told Human Rights Watch:

> This morning we handed our pamphlet out downtown [in Sittwe]. It is an announcement demanding that the Arakanese people must not sell anything to the Muslims or buy anything from them. The second point is the Arakanese people must not be friendly with the Muslim people. The reason for that is that the Muslim people are stealing our land, drinking our water, and killing our people. They are eating our rice and staying near our houses. So we will separate. We don't want any connection to the Muslim people at all.

Human Rights Watch, "'All You Can Do is Pray':
Crimes Against Humanity and Ethnic Cleansing
of Rohingya Muslims in Burma's Arakan State,"
April 2013, p. 25.

The Rohingya Have Nowhere to Go

Htun Thein, a Rohingya Muslim based in Yangon, said several boats carrying hundreds of Muslim refugees, including his sister-in-law, left Kyaukpyu on Wednesday evening headed for refugee

Anti-Muslim propaganda posters—some showing images of Buddhists killed during the 2012 violence against Muslims—hang outside a monastery in Mandalay, Burma, in 2013. © Jonas Gratzer/LightRocket via Getty Images.

camps near the state capital of Sittwe. On the way, he said, the boats were stopped by the Myanmar navy and prevented from going farther or landing.

While the passengers had some water, Htun said, they ran out of food.

A woman named Sandar delivered twins on the boat, he added in an account that could not be verified, but the lack of food and conditions aboard led to the deaths of five children including the newborns. Shine Win, a Yangon-based Muslim activist leading an interfaith group, said he hadn't heard about the dead twins but received several calls from refugees on the boats detailing children's deaths.

Khine Thurein, a Rakhine Buddhist youth activist, said the violence started Sunday when a Muslim couple quarrelled with a Rakhine man, attracting a mob that went on a rampage, burning several houses. This in turn led to reprisals over several days, he added. "It's still going on," he said. "The government is trying to control the situation, but security is limited, so it's difficult."

A statement by four Muslim groups Friday said they won't be celebrating Eid because the government can't guarantee their security.

The United Nations has called for calm, reporting that large numbers of people were seeking refuge in already overcrowded camps near Sittwe.

"The U.N. is gravely concerned about reports of a resurgence of inter-communal conflict in several areas in Rakhine state which has resulted in deaths and has forced thousands of people, including women and children, to flee their homes," Ashok Nigam, U.N. humanitarian coordinator in Myanmar, said in a statement.

Myanmar's estimated 800,000 Muslim Rohingya are officially stateless, with many among the Buddhist majority viewing them as illegal immigrants from neighboring Bangladesh. Dhaka has refused since 1992 to grant them citizenship. Rohingya say they've lived in Myanmar for generations.

"Muslims are not racist," said Abu Tahay, a Rohingya with the National Democratic Party for Development who ran for office in 1990 but was disqualified by the then-military-led government. "We just want to live peacefully."

CHAPTER 2

Controversies Surrounding the Rohingya in Burma

Chapter Exercises

"Burma—UN Finally Talks in Plain Language," cartoon by Karsten Schley, www.Cartoon Stock.com. Copyright © Karsten Schley. Reproduction rights obtainable from www.Car toonStock.com.

1. Analyze the Cartoon

Question 1: Where is the action in the cartoon taking place? How do you know? Who is the person speaking, or what does he represent? Does the artist include any clues about his identity?

Question 2: What is the attitude of the speaker toward the situation in Burma? What do you think the artist was trying to say with this cartoon? Explain.

Question 3: Write a new cartoon caption that represents what you would express about events in Burma if you were at the podium.

2. Writing Prompt

Write an editorial from the point of view of a Buddhist monk or civilian in Burma in which you argue that the Rohingya are not being subjected to genocide. Use evidence and facts from the readings in this chapter to support your argument.

3. Group Activity

In small groups develop questions that could be used by a journalist interviewing candidates for national office in Burma. The questions should be designed to clarify and illustrate how the candidate would address issues related to the Rohingya and other ethnic minorities in Burma.

The United States Supports Burma's Democratic Transformation

Barack Obama

The following viewpoint is excerpted from a speech given by US president Barack Obama. He delivered the speech in Burma a little over a year after the formal end of military dictatorship. The president praises the reforms already achieved and pledges ongoing US support for the continuing transition to greater democracy and freedom. Obama uses former US president Franklin Delano Roosevelt's four freedoms as the oratorical scaffolding for his remarks. He explains that the route to progress for Myanmar must include the freedom of expression, free assembly, and checks and balances on power; freedom from want by creating new businesses and protecting the country's natural resources; freedom of worship, including national reconciliation and the embrace of diversity; and freedom from fear for all citizens. Obama is the forty-fourth president of the United States and the recipient of the 2009 Nobel Peace Prize.

Thank you. (Applause.) Myanmar Naingan, Mingalaba [hello/greetings]! (Laughter and applause.) I am very honored to be here at this university and to be the first President of the United States of America to visit your country. . . . Above all,

Barack Obama, "Remarks by President Obama at the University of Yangon," Whitehouse.gov, November 19, 2012. www.whitehouse.gov. Courtesy of Whitehouse.gov.

I came here because of America's belief in human dignity. Over the last several decades, our two countries became strangers. But today, I can tell you that we always remained hopeful about the people of this country, about you. You gave us hope and we bore witness to your courage.

We saw the activists dressed in white visit the families of political prisoners on Sundays and monks dressed in saffron protesting peacefully in the streets. We learned of ordinary people who organized relief teams to respond to a cyclone, and heard the voices of students and the beats of hip-hop artists projecting the sound of freedom. We came to know exiles and refugees who never lost touch with their families or their ancestral home. And we were inspired by the fierce dignity of [opposition leader and activist] Daw Aung San Suu Kyi, as she proved that no human being can truly be imprisoned if hope burns in your heart.

When I took office as President, I sent a message to those governments who ruled by fear. I said, in my inauguration address, "We will extend a hand if you are willing to unclench your fist." And over the last year and a half, a dramatic transition has begun, as a dictatorship of five decades has loosened its grip. Under President Thein Sein, the desire for change has been met by an agenda for reform. A civilian now leads the government, and a parliament is asserting itself. The once-outlawed National League for Democracy stood in an election, and Aung San Suu Kyi is a Member of Parliament. Hundreds of prisoners of conscience have been released, and forced labor has been banned. Preliminary cease-fires have been reached with ethnic armies, and new laws allow for a more open economy.

Progress and the Four Freedoms

So today, I've come to keep my promise and extend the hand of friendship. America now has an Ambassador in Rangoon [Burma's largest city], sanctions have been eased, and we will help rebuild an economy that can offer opportunity for its people, and serve as an engine of growth for the world. But this remarkable journey has just begun, and has much further to go. Reforms launched from the top of society must meet the aspirations of citizens who form its foundation. The flickers of progress that we have seen must not be extinguished—they must be strengthened; they must become a shining North Star for all this nation's people.

And your success in that effort is important to the United States, as well as to me. Even though we come from different places, we share common dreams: to choose our leaders; to live together in peace; to get an education and make a good living; to love our families and our communities. That's why freedom is not an abstract idea; freedom is the very thing that makes human progress possible—not just at the ballot box, but in our daily lives.

One of our greatest Presidents in the United States, Franklin Delano Roosevelt, understood this truth. He defined America's cause as more than the right to cast a ballot. He understood democracy was not just voting. He called upon the world to embrace four fundamental freedoms: freedom of speech, freedom of worship, freedom from want, and freedom from fear. These four freedoms reinforce one another, and you cannot fully realize one without realizing them all.

So that's the future that we seek for ourselves, and for all people. And that is what I want to speak to you about today.

Freedom of Expression

First, we believe in the right of free expression so that the voices of ordinary people can be heard, and governments reflect their will—the people's will.

In the United States, for more than two centuries, we have worked to keep this promise for all of our citizens—to win freedom for those who were enslaved; to extend the right to vote for women and African Americans; to protect the rights of workers to organize.

And we recognize no two nations achieve these rights in exactly the same way, but there is no question that your country will be stronger if it draws on the strength of all of its people. That's what allows nations to succeed. That's what reform has begun to do.

Instead of being repressed, the right of people to assemble together must now be fully respected. Instead of being stifled, the veil of media censorship must continue to be lifted. And as you take these steps, you can draw on your progress. Instead of being ignored, citizens who protested the construction of the Myitsone dam were heard. Instead of being outlawed, political parties have been allowed to participate. You can see progress being made. As one voter said during the parliamentary elections here, "Our parents and grandparents waited for this, but never saw it." And now you can see it. You can taste freedom.

And to protect the freedom of all the voters, those in power must accept constraints. That's what our American system is designed to do. Now, America may have the strongest military in the world, but it must submit to civilian control. I, as the President of the United States, make determinations that the military then carries out, not the other way around. As President and Commander-In-Chief, I have that responsibility because I'm accountable to the people.

Now, on other hand, as President, I cannot just impose my will on Congress—the Congress of the United States—even though sometimes I wish I could. The legislative branch has its own powers and its own prerogatives, and so they check my power and balance my power. I appoint some of our judges, but I cannot tell them how to rule, because every person in America— from a child living in poverty to me, the President of the United States—is equal under the law. And a judge can make a determination as to whether or not I am upholding the law or breaking the law. And I am fully accountable to that law.

And I describe our system in the United States because that's how you must reach for the future that you deserve, a future where a single prisoner of conscience is one too many. You need to reach for a future where the law is stronger than any single

Aung San Suu Kyi

In 1988 Aung San Suu Kyi (born 1945) became the preeminent leader in Burma (now Myanmar) of the movement toward the reestablishment of democracy in that state. In 1991, while under house arrest, she was awarded the Nobel Peace Prize. Suu Kyi was released from her most recent house arrest term on November 13, 2010.

Aung San Suu Kyi was internationally recognized as a vibrant symbol of resistance to authoritarian rule. On July 20, 1989, she was placed under house arrest by the military coup leaders, called the State Law and Order Restoration Council (SLORC), who came to power in Myanmar on September 18, 1988, in the wake of a popular but crushed uprising against the previous, and also military headed, socialist government. The nation's name had been changed from Burma to Myanmar in 1980.

Aung San Suu Kyi came from a distinguished Burmese family. Her father, Bogyoke (Generalissimo) Aung San, is known as the founder of independent Burma in 1948 and is widely revered in that country. He negotiated independence from the British and was able to weld the diverse ethnic groups together through the force of his personality and the trust he engendered among all groups. He was assassinated, along with most of his cabinet, by a disaffected Burmese politician, U (Mr.) Saw, on July 22, 1947, prior to independence on January 4, 1948. That day remains a national remembrance holiday in Myanmar. His loss slowed the realization of state unity.

"Aung San Suu Kyi," Encyclopedia of World Biography. *Detroit, MI: Gale, 1998.*

leader, because it's accountable to the people. You need to reach for a future where no child is made to be a soldier and no woman is exploited, and where the laws protect them even if they're vulnerable, even if they're weak; a future where national security is strengthened by a military that serves under civilians and a

Constitution that guarantees that only those who are elected by the people may govern.

Freedom from Want

On that journey, America will support you every step of the way—by using our assistance to empower civil society; by engaging your military to promote professionalism and human rights; and by partnering with you as you connect your progress towards democracy with economic development. So advancing that journey will help you pursue a second freedom—the belief that all people should be free from want.

It's not enough to trade a prison of powerlessness for the pain of an empty stomach. But history shows that governments of the people and by the people and for the people are far more powerful in delivering prosperity. And that's the partnership we seek with you.

When ordinary people have a say in their own future, then your land can't just be taken away from you. And that's why reforms must ensure that the people of this nation can have that most fundamental of possessions: the right to own the title to the land on which you live and on which you work.

When your talents are unleashed, then opportunity will be created for all people. America is lifting our ban on companies doing business here, and your government has lifted restrictions on investment and taken steps to open up your economy. And now, as more wealth flows into your borders, we hope and expect that it will lift up more people. It can't just help folks at the top. It has to help everybody. And that kind of economic growth, where everybody has opportunity—if you work hard, you can succeed—that's what gets a nation moving rapidly when it comes to develop.

But that kind of growth can only be created if corruption is left behind. For investment to lead to opportunity, reform must promote budgets that are transparent and industry that is privately owned.

To lead by example, America now insists that our companies meet high standards of openness and transparency if they're doing business here. And we'll work with organizations like the World Bank to support small businesses and to promote an economy that allows entrepreneurs, small businesspeople to thrive and allows workers to keep what they earn. And I very much welcome your government's recent decision to join what we've called our Open Government Partnership, so that citizens can come to expect accountability and learn exactly how monies are spent and how your system of government operates.

Above all, when your voices are heard in government, it's far more likely that your basic needs will be met. And that's why reform must reach the daily lives of those who are hungry and those who are ill, and those who live without electricity or water. And here, too, America will do our part in working with you.

Today, I was proud to reestablish our USAID mission in this country, which is our lead development agency. And the United States wants to be a partner in helping this country, which used to be the rice bowl of Asia, to reestablish its capacity to feed its people and to care for its sick, and educate its children, and build its democratic institutions as you continue down the path of reform.

This country is famous for its natural resources, and they must be protected against exploitation. And let us remember that in a global economy, a country's greatest resource is its people. So by investing in you, this nation can open the door for far more prosperity—because unlocking a nation's potential depends on empowering all its people, especially its young people.

Just as education is the key to America's future, it is going to the be the key to your future as well. And so we look forward to working with you, as we have with many of your neighbors, to extend that opportunity and to deepen exchanges among our students. We want students from this country to travel to the United States and learn from us, and we want U.S. students to come here and learn from you.

Freedom of Worship

And this truth leads me to the third freedom that I want to discuss: the freedom to worship—the freedom to worship as you please, and your right to basic human dignity.

This country, like my own country, is blessed with diversity. Not everybody looks the same. Not everybody comes from the same region. Not everybody worships in the same way. In your cities and towns, there are pagodas and temples, and mosques and churches standing side by side. Well over a hundred ethnic groups have been a part of your story. Yet within these borders, we've seen some of the world's longest running insurgencies, which have cost countless lives, and torn families and communities apart, and stood in the way of development.

No process of reform will succeed without national reconciliation. (Applause.) You now have a moment of remarkable opportunity to transform cease-fires into lasting settlements, and to pursue peace where conflicts still linger, including in Kachin State. Those efforts must lead to a more just and lasting peace, including humanitarian access to those in need, and a chance for the displaced to return home.

Today, we look at the recent violence in Rakhine State that has caused so much suffering, and we see the danger of continued tensions there. For too long, the people of this state, including ethnic Rakhine, have faced crushing poverty and persecution. But there is no excuse for violence against innocent people. And the Rohingya hold within themselves the same dignity as you do, and I do.

National reconciliation will take time, but for the sake of our common humanity, and for the sake of this country's future, it is necessary to stop incitement and to stop violence. And I welcome the government's commitment to address the issues of injustice and accountability, and humanitarian access and citizenship. That's a vision that the world will support as you move forward.

Every nation struggles to define citizenship. America has had great debates about these issues, and those debates continue to

US president Barack Obama (center) and secretary of state Hillary Clinton (right) tour the Shwedagon Pagoda in Yangon on November 19, 2012, during the president's historic visit to Burma. © Jewel Samad/AFP/Getty Images.

this day, because we're a nation of immigrants—people coming from every different part of the world. But what we've learned in the United States is that there are certain principles that are universal, apply to everybody no matter what you look like, no matter where you come from, no matter what religion you practice: the right of people to live without the threat that their families may be harmed or their homes may be burned simply because of who they are or where they come from.

Only the people of this country ultimately can define your union, can define what it means to be a citizen of this country. But I have confidence that as you do that you can draw on this diversity as a strength and not a weakness. Your country will be stronger because of many different cultures, but you have to seize that opportunity. You have to recognize that strength.

I say this because my own country and my own life have taught me the power of diversity. The United States of America is a nation of Christians and Jews, and Muslims and Buddhists, and Hindus and non-believers. Our story is shaped by every language; it's enriched by every culture. We have people from every corner of the world. We've tasted the bitterness of civil war and segregation, but our history shows us that hatred in the human heart can recede; that the lines between races and tribes fade away. And what's left is a simple truth: e pluribus unum. . . . Out of many, we are one nation and we are one people. And that truth has, time and again, made our union stronger. It has made our country stronger. It's part of what has made America great.

We amended our Constitution to extend the democratic principles that we hold dear. And I stand before you today as President of the most powerful nation on Earth, but recognizing that once the color of my skin would have denied me the right to vote. And so that should give you some sense that if our country can transcend its differences, then yours can, too. Every human being within these borders is a part of your nation's story, and you should embrace that. That's not a source of weakness, that's a source of strength—if you recognize it.

Freedom from Fear
And that brings me to the final freedom that I will discuss today, and that is the right of all people to live free from fear.

In many ways, fear is the force that stands between human beings and their dreams. Fear of conflict and the weapons of war. Fear of a future that is different from the past. Fear of changes that are reordering our societies and economy. Fear of people who look different, or come from a different place, or worship in a different way. In some of her darkest moments, when Aung San Suu Kyi was imprisoned, she wrote an essay about freedom from fear. She said fear of losing corrupts those who wield it: "Fear of losing power corrupts those who wield it, and fear of the scourge of power corrupts those who are subject to it."

That's the fear that you can leave behind. We see that chance in leaders who are beginning to understand that power comes from appealing to people's hopes, not people's fears. We see it in citizens who insist that this time must be different, that this time change will come and will continue. As Aung San Suu Kyi wrote: "Fear is not the natural state of civilized man." I believe that. And today, you are showing the world that fear does not have to be the natural state of life in this country.

That's why I am here. That's why I came to Rangoon. And that's why what happens here is so important—not only to this region, but to the world. Because you're taking a journey that has the potential to inspire so many people. This is a test of whether a country can transition to a better place.

Burma's Democratic Transformation Is Still in Doubt

Hkun Htun Oo

The following viewpoint is by a former prisoner of conscience under the military regime who is currently the leader of Burma's largest independent ethnic party. He writes that the progress evident in the Burmese heartland is not yet seen in the more remote ethnic areas. He warns that the rule of law must be established and maintained equally throughout the country for the democratic experiment to succeed. Above all, dialogue and reconciliation are essential for a lasting peace, and he vows to assist with reforms and promote mutual understanding between the majority and minority populations. Hkun Htun Oo is chairman of the Shan Nationalities League for Democracy.

In a country whose very name is a subject of contention—Burma or Myanmar?—I confess that I'm not sure about whether we're actually witnessing democracy sprout up or not. I'm almost 70 years old; I've grown up and spent my life under military rule; and because of that, I've never experienced what it means to have basic democratic rights like freedom of expression, freedom of religion, the freedom to vote (under conditions of fair and honest competition), or the freedom of choice generally in many areas of life that people in democratic states take for granted. If one free vote is held—and only in some by-elections at that—does that amount to proof that these rights are secure and active?

The only areas in Burma where you can see towns with electricity, properly paved roads, well-staffed hospitals, industrial zones, universities with qualified teachers, five-star hotels—and no heavily armed soldiers on patrol—are in what's called *pyima*, "the main land" in the center and south of the country.

In the remote "ethnic" areas where people from non-Burman nationalities live, and where modern information technologies don't yet reach deeply, you can breathe fresh air and see mountains; but you can also see children who are malnourished and forbidden to learn in their own native languages in their own local schools. You might also see young women, trying to feed their families, who are being victimized by human traffickers, or citizens who are being displaced, either by force or to escape conflict.

These problems plague Burma's "ethnic" periphery the way that wildfires plague grasslands in the dry season. But despite 60 years of strife and conflict, those seeking to defend the rights and dignity of Burma's ethnic nationalities have remained undaunted and have kept up their fighting spirit. There's been a lot of suffering in the war-torn ethnic states of Kachin, Karen, Karenni, Mon, and Shan, but the people there have not given up hope.

Why is it that those areas where ethnic nationalities are predominant have seen such chronic violence through the military dictatorship's many decades in power? The toll has been tragic in every way: People have suffered; many have died; women have been raped; living standards have fallen; children have had to come of age without schooling.

Today, we're seeing some progress toward democracy. But I continue to worry that not all parts of the country will benefit equally from those changes. Still, I am readying myself to assist the cause of reform, not least for the sake of peace. I want to

Muslims sit in front of the ruins of their home after it was destroyed during the March 2013 riots in Mektila, Burma. Progress has been slow in the Burmese Muslim areas, compared to the "mainland." © Jonas Gratzer/LightRocket via Getty Images.

see confrontation diminish and mutual trust grow, and I will do what I can to make both those things happen.

Nobody wants to see democracy triumph more than Burma's ethnic nationalities, who have endured kinds of lifelong suffering that it would be hard for "normal" citizens to imagine. It's a common responsibility of all citizens to promote democracy's principles, to broaden democracy's scope, and to support democracy itself. In order for democracy to arise and become established, and in order for society to stay on the right path, the rule of law must be reinstated throughout the country.

Continued Dialogue Is Essential

President Thein Sein, the leader of the new administration, is trying to secure ceasefire agreements and to sign national-level peace deals with all armed organizations outside of the Burmese Communist Party. At the same time, members of parliament are calling for a lasting peace. But so far, while top officials from both sides discuss the peace process, regional units of the Burmese armed forces have continued to advance on ethnic territories. It's not a promising sign.

Our national reconciliation process can't be achieved without dialogue—including political talks. No dialogue, no reconciliation: It's that simple.

It's hard to be sanguine about our political prospects as a country so long as the most influential single force shaping our political future—namely: the current regime—remains in denial about the need for dialogue and accommodation. The regime must recognize a right to dissent. The minority must respect decisions made by the majority, and, in turn, the majority must protect the minority's rights.

As long as Burma is a diverse society made up of independent groups and organizations representing different opinions and approaches, meaningful and responsible dialogue will remain essential. Can we shun political dialogue in the hope that merely holding elections will be enough to build democracy in our country?

We can't. Just as military means haven't been the answer to the question of how to build long-term peace, elections alone won't be the answer to the question of how to build a lasting democracy. Whatever specific set of institutional answers to our problems we choose, these answers must reflect the Burmese people's desire to live in an environment characterized by fair treatment and equal opportunity for all.

In any form of democracy, freedom of choice has to be a core attribute. Above all, that's what Burma's ethnic nationalities long for. The Burmese president has said himself that he wants to see ethnic-minority youths using laptops instead of guns.

So let them choose as they wish.

The United States Should Not Support a Burmese Government That Oppresses the Rohingya

Habib Siddiqui

In the following viewpoint, a Bangladeshi expatriate in the United States expresses dismay that his adoptive country is developing a closer political and economic relationship with Burma. He writes that Burma is guilty of ongoing ethnic cleansing against the Rohingya people and cites specific examples of recent human rights violations. He urges the current Burmese government to commit to genuine democratic reform and restore basic human rights for all ethnicities in the country. He also supports the deployment of UN peacekeeping forces to make the government of Burma end ethnic cleansing. Habib Siddiqui is an antiwar and human rights activist and author. His self-published works include The Forgotten Rohingya: Their Struggle for Human Rights in Burma *and* Muslim Identity and Demography in the Arakan State of Burma (Myanmar).

Dear Mr. President [Barack Obama],

I am somewhat puzzled by your decision to visit Myanmar [Burma], which has the worst records of human rights in our planet. As an overture to your trip, your administration has

recently lifted import restrictions on Myanmar, broadly autho-
rizing Myanmar-origin goods to enter the United States for the
first time in almost a decade. So, you can understand why like so
many other concerned human rights activists, I am at a loss to
understand your rationale for the trip.

I am sure your administration is well aware of Myanmar
government's apartheid policy and its monumental crimes
against its own people, [especially] the Rohingya, who remain
the worst persecuted people in our time. The root cause of the
Rohingya people lies with the 1982 Citizenship Law, which is
at odds with scores of international laws. This law, formulated
during the hated dictator Ne Win's era, has effectively made the
Rohingya people stateless in their ancestral homeland. President
Thein Sein's quasi-civilian government promised reform from
its criminal past, but, sadly, continues to follow the footsteps of
its evil predecessors and ignore the calls from the international
community to reform or revoke that age-old racist and highly
discriminatory law.

The Myanmar government, a member of the United Nations
[UN], continues to deny human rights of the Rohingya people,
ignoring all of the thirty Articles of the Universal Declaration of
Human Rights. It is guilty of practicing a slow but steady genocidal campaign against the unarmed Rohingya civilian population, which has resulted in forced exodus of nearly two million
Rohingya people who live as unwanted refugees in many parts
of our world, including countries like Thailand and Bangladesh. While this figure of 2 million—nearly half the Rohingya
population—may not sound too large to you, but just reflect for a
moment that this is equivalent to forced expulsion of 170 million
of the U.S. population.

Surely, such a gross racism and bigotry has no place in our
time! And yet, such evil twins have become the defining charac-
teristics of today's Myanmar and its chauvinist Buddhist population. It is no accident that a Myanmar diplomat U Ye Myint Aung
working in Hong Kong called the dark brown–complexioned

Fleeing Muslim residents carry their belongings past all that remains of their community amid the June 2012 violence in Sittwe, Rakhine (Arakan) State, Burma. © STR/AFP/Getty Images.

Rohingya people "ugly as ogres." How would you, Mr. President, who is equally dark brown, have felt if such hateful comments were made about you, your wife and your children? Just take a look at the postings by racist Burmese and Rakhines [Arakanese] in the Internet to understand the depth of ugliness of today's Myanmarism. It is no accident either that [Burmese opposition leader Aung San] Suu Kyi, through her appalling silence, endorses the current extermination campaign against the Rohingya.

Mr. President, the United Nations defines ethnic cleansing as the 'purposeful policy designed by one ethnic or religious group to remove by violent and terror-inspiring means the civilian population of another ethnic or religious group from certain geographic areas.' As the never-ending episodes of violence clearly demonstrate, what the Rohingyas are facing is nothing short of ethnic cleansing by fellow Rakhines that is [supported] by state security forces, politicians, and government officers.

Ethnic cleansing of the Rohingya people has truly become a national project in today's Myanmar that enjoys wide support from within the Buddhist population. In recent months [as of

November 2012], the Rakhine Buddhist terrorists and their pa-
trons and partners-in-crime within the government—central
and local—have uprooted more than a hundred thousand Rohingya people, let alone torched hundreds of Rohingya villages
and townships. Muslim parts of the most of the towns and cities within the Rakhine [Arakan] state have simply been wiped
out, as if they are bombed out places reminiscent of the Second
World War. With homes, shops, schools, businesses, mosques,
crops and cattle burned down, the Rohingya people are forced to
either risk the high seas to seek a shelter anywhere or settle for
segregated prison-like concentrations camps outside [state capi-
tal] Sittwe (Akyab) in the Rakhine state. Regrettably, the Government of Bangladesh continues to deny them shelter. In recent
days, hundreds have died in the Bay of Bengal. Thousands have
also died as a result of the latest genocidal campaign.

Deemed stateless by the ultra-racist 1982 Citizenship Law,
where will the Rohingya go and who will shelter them? What excuse does the world community, especially the powerful nations
like the USA, have to stop this greatest crime committed by the
Myanmar government and its racist elements within the society
in our time?

Mr. President, please, read US photographer Greg Constantine's recently released book *Exiled to Nowhere: Burma's Rohingya* to understand their human stories. He relates the story
of 20-year-old Kashida who had to flee to Bangladesh with her
husband. The Burmese authorities had denied her permission
to get married, but when they discovered she had married in secret and was pregnant they took away all her family's money and
cows and goats. They forced Kashida to have an abortion, telling
her: "This is not your country; you don't have the right to repro-
duce here." What atrocity and what brutality, and yet no relief for
this unfortunate people! Rape has become a weapon of war to
terrorize this people.

President Thein Sein is guilty of speaking with a forked
tongue. He reneged on his agreement with the OIC [Organisa-

tion of Islamic Cooperation]. He is averse to international observers and an independent UN Commission of Inquiry. He likes to hide his regime's crimes. He is not serious about securing the lives and properties of the non-Buddhist Rohingya people.

Last Friday, 3,000 Rakhine Buddhist terrorists surrounded the village of Paik Thae in Kyauktaw Township [in Rakhine] to evict the Muslim inhabitants. On Saturday morning some 200 security forces and Burmese Army soldiers entered the Muslim village of Anaryme in Pauktaw and ordered the Muslim villagers to leave their houses and the village. They have evicted these Muslims from their homes so that the security forces and soldiers can live in them. How can our generation allow such crimes of forced eviction?

As I write on Saturday [November 17, 2012], 50 ponds in Rohingya villages of U Hla Pe and Rwa Nyo Daung in Buthidaung Township have been found to be poisoned by Rakhine terrorists. It was aimed at killing the Rohingyas of those villages who depend on those ponds for drinking water.

Dear Mr. President, the list of such daily abuse, harassment, persecution and slow but steady genocidal campaign to wipe out the Rohingya and Muslim identity of Arakan and Myanmar is long and simply unacceptable. It needs to be stopped. Your visit to Myanmar should not and cannot be interpreted as an endorsement of the devious policies of the Thein Sein government which wants to push out the Rohingya minorities one way or another.

I, therefore, urge you to press President Thein Sein for genuine democratic reform, national reconciliation and restoration of human rights, and an end to [the] genocidal campaign against the Rohingya and grant them citizenship on par with other ethnic nationalities.

I urge you to insist that if the Myanmar government is desirous of a friendly relationship with the USA, it must allow safe, timely and unhindered access of international media and rights groups across the Rakhine (Arakan) state to monitor and thus, act as a deterrent to any future pogrom against the Rohingya minorities. It must support UN peace-keeping forces being sent to Arakan for the purpose of preventing final solution of the Rohingya problem. It must also allow the UN to conduct unbiased inquiry and to send independent international observers to the troubled region. Like the Rohingyas in the Rakhine state, some 90,000 people have also been internally displaced in the Kachin state who are denied humanitarian aid by the Thein Sein regime. Therefore, you must stress the urgent need to allow international aid to reach the Rohingya and other affected minorities for security conditions that would allow them to return to their homes safely. The Myanmar government must also compensate the victims.

In 1994, Rwanda witnessed genocide in which more than half a million Tutsis were killed. The [former US president Bill] Clinton administration did not act quickly enough after the killing began and failed to call the crimes by their rightful name: genocide. Four years later, President Clinton and the First Lady Hillary Rodham Clinton visited the capital city of Kigali to apologize for the international community's failure to stop the genocide. I pray and hope that we shall be spared of a repeat of that sad episode of American indecision to come to the rescue of an endangered people.

Mr. President, the Rohingyas are victims of genocide in Myanmar. No linguistic camouflage of the yesteryears can hide this ugly truth. Please, have the moral authority to call a spade a spade, and stop this genocide, failing which, I am afraid, the Rohingyas will be an extinct community. Simply put, the human rights of the Rohingya and other affected minorities cannot take a backseat when they face extermination. It would be the greatest crime under your watch! Please, stop the extinction of the Rohingyas of Myanmar.

Sincerely,
Habib Siddiqui

The World Is Ignoring the Rohingya Genocide

Nancy Hudson-Rodd

In the following viewpoint, a human rights researcher who specializes in Burma writes that government-sanctioned persecution of the Rohingya continues undeterred. She writes that demands for investigations by the United Nations have been ignored, and the Burmese government denies and covers up reports of violence. The government also refuses to revise the "national races" law that sanctions behavior that is tantamount to ethnic cleansing, according to human rights and genocide watchdog groups. The author writes that the lack of response from Western countries while the destruction of the Rohingya continues is similar to that of bystander nations during the early years of the Holocaust in Nazi Germany. Nancy Hudson-Rodd is an Australian scholar, an honorary research fellow at Edith Cowan University, and an associate at the University of Tasmania.

On January 23 [2014], the United Nations [UN] Special Rapporteur on Human Rights in Myanmar [Burma] and humanitarian chiefs voiced "deep concern" on reports of "alarming levels of violence" against ethnic Rohingya in Myanmar's western Rakhine [Arakan] State. When their houses were being robbed in DuChiraDan village, Maungdaw, the Rohingya residents called for help, according to reports. The villagers fled the site when they realized that the robbers included police and ethnic Rakhine extremists.

At 3 AM that morning, a group of military, other security forces, and police raided the village, blocked the entrance, and fired indiscriminately on escaping men, women, and children. At least 40 people were killed and many more injured. The remaining villagers were rounded up, put into two trucks, and carried off to an unknown location. Authorities later declared the village a "no-entry zone".

The UN Rapporteur demanded the government immediately investigate the reports of violence. This call was ignored, as have been all the other "urgent" calls for action by various international groups. Instead, the Ministry of Information announced that journalists responsible for reporting the story would be held accountable for any "unrest" in Rakhine State supposedly caused by their reports.

Denials and Cover-Ups by the Government

The government's media mouthpiece, [English-language newspaper] *New Light of Myanmar*, ran an article claiming false reports of violence, citing a Maungdaw policeman who denied any incidents occurred. The article concluded that "reports of killings caused by racial and religious conflicts seemed to instigate unrest".

Ethnic Rohingya are not recognized as one of Myanmar's 135 "official national races". According to the UN, they are one of the world's most persecuted minority groups. The UN refused a Myanmar minister's request in 2011 to resettle to second countries all of the estimated 800,000 Rohingya now resident in Myanmar.

President Thein Sein, meanwhile, refuses to amend the 1982 law which stripped all Rohingya of their citizenship. He recently asserted: "the law is meant to protect the country and the government has no plans to revise it". A census to be completed in 2014 has no category for the Rohingya, only Bengali, an exercise that will effectively erase the minority group's existence from the country.

Government Sanctioned Persecution

The Rohingya's lack of legal status effectively gives state approval to endemic discrimination. Thein Sein claims sectarian, religious or ethnic tensions are an "unwelcome by-product" of political liberalization. Such official deflections deny the state's involvement in the unfolding genocide now taking place in Myanmar.

They also build upon dangerous psychological and ideological factors that have induced violent grassroots reactions to racist rumors and claims against Rohingya. *Progress Magazine*, the official journal of the Rakhine Nationalities Development Party, openly wrote (November 2012) of ridding Myanmar of its Rohingya population. The magazine wrote:

> [Adolf] Hitler and [Adolf] Eichmann were the enemy of the Jews, but were probably heroes to the Germans. . . . In order for a country's survival, the survival of a race, or in defense of national sovereignty, crimes against humanity or in-human acts may justifiably be committed as Hitler and the Holocaust. If that survival principle or justification is applied or permitted equally (in our Myanmar case) our endeavors to protect our Rakhine race and defend the sovereignty and longevity of the Union of Myanmar cannot be labelled as "crimes against humanity", or "inhuman" or "in-humane". . . . We no longer wish to hold permanent concerns about the Bengali in our midst. We just want to get it over and done with, once and for all.

Along that editorial line, Myanmar has witnessed unprecedented pogroms and riots against Rohingya since the summer of 2012. They have been systematically uprooted, with 140,000 held in internal displacement camps and unknown thousands have taken to sea as refugees. Their homes, businesses, and mosques have been destroyed. Amid the destruction, many Rohingya have been unfairly imprisoned, with some tortured to death while behind bars.

The UN Rapporteur has urged Thein Sein to release two prominent Rohingya prisoners of conscience, community leaders Dr Tun Aung and Kyaw Hla Aung. Both have been falsely charged, denied lawyers, refused medical care, held incommunicado, and referred to in racist terms. Instead, Thein Sein has denied the UN's and other groups' claims of widespread, systemic, and state-supported acts of violence against Rohingya. He has conducted no independent investigation into the spreading violence, held no person accountable for the deaths and destruction, and denied holding prisoners of conscience.

Grave Concern Among Genocide Watchdog Groups

Gregory Stanton, president of Genocide Watch, a nongovernmental organization, describes genocide as a process that develops in 10 not necessarily sequential stages, with many occurring at the same time. As defined by this 10-point metric and determined by the Toronto-based Project for Genocide Prevention, Myanmar is at extremely high risk of full-blown genocide.

For instance, there is a proliferation of internally displaced persons (IDP) camps in Rakhine State. Sealed-off ghettoes within urban areas constitute by some definitions genocide by isolation, starvation, and deprivation of the necessities of life, if done with the intent to destroy the group. The Rohingya are being systematically purged from towns, villages, and cities throughout Rakhine State and elsewhere across the country.

This purge is being hidden from the outside world. The government asks for and receives international funds under the guise of humanitarian help for Rohingya, yet does not allow aid workers to visit all the IDP camps. In November 2013, when the European Commission promised to increase humanitarian support to Myanmar, they issued a statement likening conditions for

Rohingya held in IDP camps in Rakhine State, to those of Jewish people in ghettoes established by Nazi-run Germany. Australia is the largest funder, giving US$8,410,411 of humanitarian assistance as of January 2014.

In [the] book *Genocide: A Critical Bibliographic Review*, Leo Kuper explains that nations will continue to express their optimism about certain governments' reforms despite abundant evidence about continued systematic repression. Thein Sein's abusive policies, cloaked in terms of democratization and political reform, are openly supported by many Western governments.

The term "bystander nation" was originally used to describe Allied governments' lack of response to early knowledge of the unfolding destruction of European Jews, the reluctance to believe allegations of genocide, and the refusal to adopt policies for action. Today, genocide is an unfolding reality in Myanmar and the complicit silence of Western donor nations is deafening.

Using Terms Like "Genocide" Will Worsen the Plight of the Rohingya

Kyaw San Wai

The following viewpoint is by a researcher at a university in Burma focusing on strategic and international affairs in the Asia Pacific. The author writes that ethnic violence in the western part of the country has subsided. However, partisan portrayals of the conflict between the Rohingya and the majority ethnic Arakanese, or Rakhine, jeopardize the security of locals and Burma's reform process. He explains that the biased portrayals are driven by politics and religion and have given the Rohingya the upper hand in the media war. He also warns that such media bias may lead to a radicalized Muslim population. The fragile reform process, he concedes, can only move forward if both sides approach each other with respect and willingness to compromise. Kyaw San Wai is a senior analyst in the dean's office of the S. Rajaratnam School of International Studies and focuses on biosecurity in the school's Science, Technology, and Security Programme.

The violence which flared up in Western Myanmar [Burma] appears to have died down. However, the Rohingyas' allegations that they bore the brunt of the government's security operations have led to a growing call from Muslim countries and organisations for intervention in Myanmar. The country's fragile transition to democracy has further complicated the picture, as public opinion and a freer press come into play in an extremely sensitive issue. With different portrayals galvanizing various involved and uninvolved communities, there is a risk of the situation taking on extremist dimensions.

Politics and Religion Drive Portrayals in the Media

The Arakanese and Rohingyas have accused each other of premeditated and organised violence. During the unrests, the violent behaviour of one to the other was meticulously reported, with a de facto competition to upload grisly photos of victims online. Eye witness accounts, sourced and used selectively by both sides, differed wildly. Such accounts, though extremely difficult to verify, were readily utilised and embellished. The Arakanese received sympathy from the Burmese press, while the Rohingya appeared to have the upper hand abroad in the 'media war' aspect of the unrests.

The portrayal of the conflict has varied greatly and is seen as reflecting the political (and religious) stance of the reporting agencies. Burmese non-state media had generally framed the situation mainly as an 'immigrant vs. host' situation instigated by the Rohingya. Western media had been trotting out the line of sectarian conflict where the 'Buddhist Arakanese' were pitted against the 'Muslim Rohingya'. Arakanese groups, based mainly inside Myanmar, have portrayed it as a Rohingya instigated conflict. Pictures and videos of Arakanese and ostensibly non-Rohingya Muslim refugees and victims recounting Rohingya perpetrated violence, reports of arms cache finds in Rohingya villages and of armed men arriving in boats from Bangladesh, have circulated widely among Burmese circles.

A plethora of overseas Rohingya organisations increasingly have framed the situation as a government orchestrated, religiously motivated genocide against Burmese Muslims. Most

The United States Strikes the Right Balance in Myanmar

The situation in Rakhine state is a difficult one for the Myanmar government and is therefore one that the international community must broach sensitively. From the Myanmar government's perspective, it is caught between a rock and a hard place. Even if it had the political will to help the Rohingya (there appears to be little with the 2015 election looming and widespread anti-Rohingya sentiment in the country), it would have difficulty persuading the Rakhine and the broader populace to accept this. The Rakhine are said to hate the Burmans almost as much as they despise the Rohingya, so the government has little, if any persuasive sway. The U.S. embassy in Myanmar appears, broadly, to be striking the right balance between urging the government to address the dire situation in Rakhine state and understanding the constraints it faces.

Apart from humanitarian assistance, the United States' focus in the short-term should be on working behind the scenes to keep up the pressure on the Myanmar government to grand individual Rohingya citizenship and the rights that accompany it. This would admittedly benefit only a small number—Naypyidaw recently categorically rejected the United Nations' call to give the Rohingya full access to citizenship—but it would at least be a start.

According to the report of the government's commission on violence in Rakhine state, most Rakhine accept that "Bengalis" who fit the legal criteria for citizenship should be given it, though they oppose the claim of "Bengalis who wish to be labeled . . . one of the indigenous groups of the Union of Myanmar." The weak appetite for recognizing the Rohingya as a community is replicated outside of Rakhine, even among those who might generally be sympathetic to their situation. Part of the reason for this is a fear that it would pave the way for other communities like the Chinese and Indians to also make claims to be recognized.

Lynn Kuok, Promoting Peace in Myanmar: US Interests and Role. *Lanham, MD: Rowman & Littlefield, 2014, p. 26.*

estimates hover at around 80 deaths and 90,000 displaced persons and thousands of homes burnt, from both sides. However, some media and Islamist groups have interpreted that all deaths, destruction and refugees were only among the Rohingya community.

Muslim online opinion expressed on the issue has also generally framed it as a genocide directed against all Myanmar Muslims. The Burmese are portrayed as inherently racist and Islamophobic, and the argument is unfortunately strengthened by acerbic online responses from Burmese netizens. Claims that over 20,000 Muslims have been killed in the recent violence have also spread on some Muslim websites. Pictures claimed to be of masses of Rohingya corpses have also circulated online. However, these pictures appeared to be recycled ones of Rohingya refugees detained by Thai or Indonesian security personnel.

This last narrative has been picked up by media outlets in some Muslim countries, based on which some Islamic organisations, including the Organisation of Islamic Cooperation, have started calling for intervention on behalf of the Rohingya. Protests were held outside Myanmar missions in Egypt and Kuwait while around 300 Islamic hardliners vowed jihad in front of the Burmese embassy in Jakarta [Indonesia] on 13 July [2012].

Potential for Islamic Radicalization

The Arakanese and Burmese have labelled the Rohingya rioters as terrorists operating on the instructions of Al Qaeda [a radical Islamic terrorist organization]. While this is highly unlikely, there have been attempts by certain Rohingya organisations in the past to link up with regional militant Islamic organisations with links to the Taliban [in Afghanistan] and Al Qaeda, and Rohingya militant training camps and Rohingyas receiving militant training have been documented.

As these activities have been relatively minor and isolated, it is highly unlikely that most of Rohingya society has undergone radicalisation. However, with poverty, a lack of political alternatives, pervasive prejudice and possible instigation from 'interested' extremists, the continuing lack of solution to the Rohingya situation can serve to fuel segments of Rohingya society to pursue a violent path. The real and embellished accounts, genuine and doctored photos, alongside rumours online may galvanize extremist groups unconnected with Myanmar to carry out 'retaliatory' attacks.

There appears to be a distinct line drawn between other Muslims in Myanmar and the Rohingya in the Burmese perspective – the 'sentiment' has been anti-Rohingya rather than anti-Muslim. However, calls for action from Islamic countries and organisations, and extremist reactions, could very well erode this barrier and unleash a wider religious conflict. Thus far, the violence has been limited to Rakhine [Arakan] State; the Burmese government, as well as Buddhist, Muslim and other organisations have been working to prevent the problem from spreading further.

A Rohingya family rests at Thae Chaung refugee camp on the outskirts of Sittwe, Burma, in 2012. Some believe that biased portrayals in the media will lead to a radicalized Muslim population. © Kaung Htet/Getty Images.

Compromise and Communication Will Ensure Reforms

Solving the situation would take time, effort, education, discussions and compromise. Addressing the Citizenship Law [the Burmese statute denying the Rohingya citizenship], improving the overall economic and social situation of Rakhine State and tackling demographic issues would be some of the steps crucial to diffusing the tension. As both sides argue incessantly on the basis of history, clarifying the region's history might also help to some extent.

Separating the two communities, as the government has currently done for short-term security reasons, would temporarily alleviate the violence but will only reinforce mutual distrust in the long run. Involvement by uninformed external parties galvanized by embellished statements would only serve to further complicate a delicate solution. The Burmese government, used to quelling such incidents through force, is only starting to figure out how to settle such matters without the gun and by properly addressing human security issues.

There is no debate on the situation—civilised communication is lacking and the Arakanese and the Rohingya are pathologically dismissive of the other's notions, usually on ad hominem bases. The unrest risks derailing the fragile reform process, as it augments arguments for a return to authoritarianism. The situation in Western Myanmar will prove to be a serious challenge not only for Naypyidaw [the Burmese capital], but also for neighbouring governments.

Standards of International Justice Could Help the Rohingya

Sam Zarifi

In the following viewpoint, a human rights expert expresses dismay that human rights workers in Burma deny those very rights to the Rohingya. He cites blatantly racist sentiments that are believed about the Muslim minority and reports on the long history of abuses against them, beginning with the 1982 Citizenship Law. He explains that even former political prisoner and human rights icon Aung San Suu Kyi does not speak out against Rohingya discrimination. Because Burma's government is unwilling to address ethnic and sectarian tensions that impede economic and political progress, it is up to the international community to force Burma to apply human rights standards for all its people. Sam Zarifi is the regional director for Asia and Oceania at the International Commission of Jurists. From 2010 to 2012 he was Amnesty International's Asia-Pacific director.

An awkward silence in a small restaurant in Yangon [largest city in Burma]: The veteran dissident and pro-democracy activist had just explained why he does not have much sympathy for the Rohingya despite the widespread and systematic violence they have faced, because, as he saw it, "Rohingya" is a "made up name" and "they are all illegal immigrants from Bangladesh and they should go back there."

He is not at all unique. During our recent visits to Burma—now called Myanmar by its government—we heard this blatantly racist sentiment repeatedly, including from lawyers and activists who apparently saw no contradiction between demanding human rights and greater rights for the country's beleaguered ethnic minorities while, at the same time, denying such rights to the Rohingya.

Two weeks ago [September 2012], even Buddhist monks marched in downtown Yangon to demand expulsion of the Rohingya.

It is difficult to change such attitudes by confronting them directly, as tempting as it may be. What we have found is that a better response is pointing to international human rights standards—the same standards that many dissidents and activists in Myanmar have been invoking in their own defense—and explaining that these standards should be applied to all, regardless of their ethnicity or legal status.

It is crucial for the Myanmar government, as well as opposition leader Aung San Suu Kyi, to publicly announce—and demonstrate—their commitment to these standards and begin the work of getting public acceptance for them, for all people living in Myanmar.

A Long Record of Abuses

The discrimination against the Rohingya has been egregious in Myanmar for years, as they have been rendered stateless under the country's 1982 Citizenship Law, which denies them Myanmar citizenship and thus severely curtails their right to hold property, or enter school, or even get married.

Most recently the issue has gained increased urgency because of bloody clashes between the Muslim Rohingya and Buddhists in resource-rich Arakan state.

According to reports from credible sources, including To-mas Quintana, the UN's Special Rapporteur on the situation in Myanmar, armed gangs from both communities killed dozens, burned down several villages, and displaced tens of thousands of people while government security forces stood by, or worse, in some cases targeted the Rohingya.

In the face of such virulence, even Aung San Suu Kyi, the human rights icon and Nobel Peace laureate, has been uncomfortably ambiguous, calling only for 'the rule of law' to determine the Rohingya's citizenship status. Her perceived silence has tarnished her halo, as international observers have criticized her for failing to stand up for the rights of a historically abused minority group.

Internal Constraints to Reconciliation

From inside the country, however, Aung San Suu Kyi's vacillation is more easily understood (though not excused). At this point she is a clear beneficiary (and somewhat surprising co-sponsor) of the remarkable reforms pushed by President Thein Sein. She is a member of parliament now, which her party, the National League for Democracy, has every expectation of dominating if open elections are held. She is also viewed as a strong candidate for the country's leadership, should the reform process continue.

In such a position, she is severely constrained in what she can say to maintain her support among her political base and future voters. The Buddhist monks who marched in Yangon against the Rohingya were mostly drawn from a faction of activist monks who have supported Aung San Suu Kyi in her opposition to the government (most notably during the 2007 'Saffron Revolution'), but were also noted for consistently advocating violence against Muslims. They would likely press Aung San Suu Kyi strenuously to avoid any conciliatory language.

The hatred against the Rohingya is most pronounced, but a quick glance at media inside the country, now freer from government constraints, shows that racism is already prevalent and growing: there are frequent attempts to cast Chinese migrants allegedly entering Kachin State, or Indians from Manipur, as scapegoats for economic problems or the drug trade.

Myanmar's government understands, as well as Aung San Suu Kyi, that ethnic and sectarian tensions pose a serious threat to the country's economic development and its reform process. As hard as it may be, both Aung San Suu Kyi and the government must begin to curb this problem immediately.

The Need for International Pressure

This is precisely where international law and standards can be of immense value. There is enormous desire inside the country to end the country's isolation, and a major part of that is cleaning up the country's terrible human rights record.

One of the bedrock principles of international human rights is that governments cannot discriminate on the basis of religion or national origin. This is one of the pillars of international law, including the UN Charter and the Universal Declaration of Human Rights. Notwithstanding the legal status of the Rohingya, or any other ethnic and religious groups, they are protected by international law, and the government of Myanmar is obliged to protect their rights.

Myanmar's leaders must begin publicly embracing these standards. Moreover, pro-democracy activists and human rights defenders within the country must also start realizing and begin to acknowledge that the same standards that were invoked to protect tens of thousands of refugees and asylum seekers from Myanmar in neighboring countries, such as Thailand, China, and India, also apply inside the country's borders.

Public information campaigns about human rights thus would benefit both the government as well as the political opposition.

There are still tremendous human rights problems in Myanmar, ranging from incarceration of political critics and disbarring of activist lawyers, to war crimes in the grinding internal conflicts between the army and armed ethnic groups, to massive institutional failure to alleviate the country's crushing poverty and high rates of maternal and infant mortality. But there is hope now that these problems can be addressed if the current trend toward reforms continues.

The people of Myanmar would greatly benefit from understanding that these rights apply to all, regardless of ethnicity or citizenship, and that their government will demonstrate in practice its commitment to implement these rights.

Compromise and Resettlement Could Help the Rohingya

Nehginpao Kipgen

In the following viewpoint, a member of a Tibeto-Burman tribal group writes about the escalation of tensions in 2013 between the Rohingya and the ethnic majority in Arakan State. He explains that Western powers have not paid serious attention to sectarian violence, while Muslim nations allege that the Rohingya are persecuted because of their religion. However, according to the author, the root of the problem stems from the uncertain legal status of the Rohingya, who are considered illegal immigrants by the Burmese government. Possible solutions described in the viewpoint include resettlement, integration, or citizenship for the Rohingya. Nehginpao Kipgen is general secretary of the United States–based Kuki International Forum and has written many articles on the politics of Burma and Asia.

Since May this year [2013], Myanmar [Burma]has witnessed an escalation in the simmering tension between two groups of people in Rakhine State. The violence between the Rakhine (also known as Arakan) and Rohingya (also known as Bengali) has led to the death of at least 88 people and displacement of thousands of others. Unofficial reports, however, put the number of deaths in the hundreds.

The immediate cause of the violence was the rape and murder of a Rakhine Buddhist woman on May 28 by three male Rohingya. This was followed by a retaliatory killing of 10 Muslims by a mob of Rakhine on June 3. It should be noted that tension between these two groups has existed for several decades.

Several questions are being routinely asked: Why has little apparently been done to resolve the conflict? Is there a possibility of reaching a permanent solution to this protracted problem? Much blame has also been directed at both the Myanmar government and the opposition, led by Daw Aung San Suu Kyi.

Mixed International Response

As members of the international community are trying to promote their own national interests in newly democratic Myanmar, sectarian violence such as we have seen in Rakhine State has not been paid serious attention, especially by Western powers.

While Human Rights Watch has criticised the Myanmar government for failing to prevent the initial unrest, majority Muslim nations, such as Indonesia, Egypt, Saudi Arabia, Pakistan and Malaysia have criticised what they allege is discrimination against the Rohingya based on their religious beliefs.

The sensitivity of the issue has silenced many from discussing it publicly. Even the internationally acclaimed human rights champion and leader of the democratic opposition, Daw Aung San Suu Kyi, has made only brief comments about the conflict, emphasising the need to establish an adequate citizenship law.

Citizenship Status as the Root of the Problem

The root of the problem begins with the nomenclature itself. Although many of the Muslims in Rakhine State call themselves Rohingya, the Myanmar government and many of the country's citizens call them illegal Bengali migrants from neighbouring Bangladesh.

Thein Sein

Though the election results were disappointing, a week after the vote in November 2010, the generals unexpectedly released Suu Kyi from house arrest. Then Than Shwe decided to retire, to be replaced by another high-ranking general Thein Sein, who had previously served as Prime Minister. He would put away his uniform and lead a nominally civilian government. Unlike other members of the regime, Thein Sein had traveled around the region, was well known to Asian diplomats, and had seen firsthand how Burma's neighbors were enjoying the benefits of trade and technology while his own country stagnated. Rangoon had once been one of the more cosmopolitan cities in Southeast Asia; Thein Sein knew just how far it now lagged behind places like Bangkok, Jakarta, Singapore, and Kuala Lumpur. According to the World Bank, in 2010 only 0.2 percent of the country's population used the Internet. Smartphones were nonexistent because there was insufficient cellular service. The contrast to their neighbors could not have been starker.

Hillary Rodham Clinton, Hard Choices: A Memoir. *New York: Simon & Schuster, 2014, p. 103.*

Since the governments of Myanmar and Bangladesh have refused to accept them as their citizens, the Rohingya have automatically become stateless under international law. Under such circumstances, are there any possible solutions to the problem?

President U Thein Sein suggested that the United Nations High Commissioner for Refugees (UNHCR) should consider resettling the Rohingya in other countries. Although such proposal may sound ideal to many, there would definitely be challenges in terms of implementation.

For example, will there be a nation or nations willing to welcome and embrace the million or so Rohingya people? Moreover, UNHCR chief António Guterres has rejected the idea of resettlement. Even if the agency reconsidered its position, would

Smoke rises from burning buildings during riots in Meiktila, Burma, on March 21, 2013. The escalation of violence is partly due to the uncertain legal status of the Rohingya, who are considered illegal residents. © Mantharlay/AFP/Getty Images.

the UNHCR offices in Myanmar and Bangladesh have adequate resources to process such a large number of people?

Potential Solutions

One possible solution is for the governments of Myanmar and Bangladesh to reach an amicable arrangement to integrate the Rohingya population into their respective societies. There are about 800,000 Rohingya inside Myanmar and another 300,000 in Bangladesh.

This proposition also has its own challenges. Chiefly, will the indigenous Rakhine accept Rohingya as their fellow citizens and live peacefully with them? On the other hand, will the Bangladesh government change its policy and offer citizenship to the Rohingya?

Another possible solution is that Myanmar can amend its 1982 citizenship law to pave the way for the Rohingya to apply for citizenship. As Minister for Immigration and Population U Khin

Yi told Radio Free Asia recently, under the existing law foreigners can apply for citizenship only if they are born in Myanmar, their parents and grandparents have lived and died in Myanmar, they are literate in Burmese and meet some additional criteria.

Finally, to prevent a further escalation in tensions, the governments of Myanmar and Bangladesh need to secure their porous international borders to prevent illegal movements.

None of the above suggested policies are simple and easy to achieve. Despite the challenges and difficulties, the Rohingya issue cannot be ignored for too long. Without addressing the crux of the problem, the May incident and the violence it sparked could recur, with even more tragic consequences.

Until a solution is achieved, international institutions, such as the United Nations and Association of Southeast Asian Nations, should pressure the Myanmar government to take steps to resolve the problem of Rohingya statelessness in a holistic manner, rather than inciting, or allowing others to incite, hatred along religious or racial lines.

Religious Conflict Fuels Anti-Rohingya Violence

Francis Wade

In the following viewpoint, a British newspaper reports that religious animosity fuels ethnic violence in Burma. According to the author, both Muslims and Buddhists describe attacks on their villages by people of the other religion. While the tensions between the two religions have festered for decades, the author writes, they are complicated by the more recent history of Burmese nationalism. The author explains that until recently, Rohingya and Buddhists mingled freely, but now many Muslims live in ghettos, some having been displaced from their home villages. Unfortunately, both sides have failed to cooperate in investigations into the violence and with a commission set up to look into the unrest. (Note: Some of the names of individuals in the viewpoint were changed for security reasons.) Francis Wade is a freelance journalist, photographer, and videographer based in Thailand. His writing on Burma and Southeast Asia has appeared in The Guardian, *the* Los Angeles Review of Books, Foreign Policy, Time, *Al Jazeera English, and other publications.*

Khamal Alam is the only member of his family to survive the recent violence in western Burma. The 25-year-old from the

Rohingya minority says all his relatives were shot by government troops who opened fire on the Muslims during running battles with the Buddhist Arakanese.

Alam arrived at the Thae Chaung refugee camp after fleeing his home town of Kyaukphyu when several hundred houses were burned by local Buddhists. "Nobody died from the sword, only gunshots," said another Kyaukphyu resident now in the camp.

Hundreds of Muslim Rohingya people have been killed and tens of thousands displaced in recent weeks in renewed clashes with the Arakan Buddhists. But where there is conflict there are always two sides to the story.

Ko Aye, 14, a Buddhist from Yaithein village, last saw his 15-year-old friend lying on the ground, bleeding from a sword wound just below his neck. A mob had descended on his village, razing the homes of the largely Buddhist community. "Hundreds of Muslims arrived carrying bows, swords and fire torches," he recalled of that morning, before he and his family fled. "I was on the street, and everyone ran as they began burning houses."

The violence between the Rohingya Muslims and the Arakan Buddhists has raised fresh questions about Burma's reform process at a time when the country is flirting with opening up to the outside world.

With Barack Obama due to visit the country in a fortnight [November 2012], renewed scrutiny will be placed on Washington's warming relations with the [Burmese president] Thein Sein administration. "He absolutely has to raise the issue [of the Rohingya]," said Chris Lewa, head of the Arakan Project, a Thailand-based NGO monitoring abuses in western Burma. "It's a great opportunity to press the government on the 1982 citizenship law [which denies the Rohingya citizenship]. It would be disappointing if he didn't."

Tensions Between Buddhists and Muslims

The unrest, which first engulfed large parts of Arakan state in June after the rape of an Arakanese woman by three Rohingya men was reported, resumed three weeks ago. A state of emergency has been in place since the summer, and access to affected areas is difficult. *The Guardian* was denied permission to visit Yaithein village, where witnesses of the violence tell of beheadings and incinerated bodies, and where a heavy troop presence blocks accurate assessment of the magnitude of the situation.

Tensions between Buddhists and Muslims have festered for decades here: both have suffered abuse from the government, but have directed their response largely at one another. Arakanese blame aggressive attempts to stamp a Burman identity on the state as reason for a fierce nationalism. The target of this has often been the Rohingya, whom both Arakanese and the government claim are illegal immigrants from Bangladesh. U Nya Nya, chairman of a monks' association in Sittwe, says the Rohingya identity was only adopted in the 1950s as "an attempt by illegal Bengalis" to get recognition as a distinct ethnic group in Burma. Historical references, such as a 1799 study of dialects by ethnographer Francis Buchanan which refers to the "Rooinga", are dismissed by Arakanese, and anti-Rohingya sentiments have conspired to render the group stateless: they are denied citizenship and suffer tight restrictions on their movement.

An Apartheid-Like State for the Rohingya

Aung Mingalar is the last surviving Muslim district in Sittwe, and in many ways embodies the dark heart of the conflict. Barbed wire barricades manned by soldiers mark the entrance to this ghetto. Few of its 8,000 inhabitants, mostly Rohingya, dare to leave, while Arakanese taxi drivers go only as far as the checkpoints. Until June, Rohingya and Buddhists in Sittwe mingled freely, but now both fear attacks as they pass through one another's neighbourhoods.

"I would not be surprised if the local Arakanese population attempt to drive out Aung Mingalar residents, and soon," said Matthew Smith, a researcher at Human Rights Watch. "They've

Enraged Buddhism

Some might be surprised to hear of conflict between Buddhists and Muslims in Burma. The common view in the West is that Buddhism is a religion of inward contemplation and perhaps inactivity. Buddhism, however, like other religions, is implicated in everyday, worldly affairs.

Two of the realities of contemporary Buddhism in Asia are what is described by some scholars as 'engaged Buddhism' and 'enraged Buddhism'. First emerging in the nineteenth century and popularized by Vietnamese Monk Thich Nhat Hanh in the 1960s, 'engaged Buddhism' refers to Buddhists' 'energetic engagement with social and political issues and crises'. The most conspicuous examples of engaged Buddhism include Nobel Peace Prize recipient the [Fourteenth] Dalai Lama, who has campaigned internationally for his country of Tibet, and Burmese politician Aung San Suu Kyi who has vociferously and bravely opposed the ruling military in her home country.

Buddhism is involved in politics in other ways. Although not as numerous as Hindu nationalist movements, there has been a rise in Buddhist nationalist political groups in recent decades. They campaign on a religious-nationalist agenda (where religious identity serves as the basis for nationhood). The rise of Buddhist nationalists is connected to ethnic-religious conflict and tensions in specific countries. A notable example is Sri Lanka, where there has been an active Sinhalese-Buddhist nationalist movement opposed to Hindu Tamils. Outbreaks of religiously motivated violence, like that in Burma, are described by some commentators as instances of 'enraged Buddhism'. Both engaged and enraged Buddhism are responses to the contemporary social world in which Buddhists live.

Andrew Singleton, Religion, Culture, and Society: A Global Approach. *Thousand Oaks, CA: Sage, 2014, pp. 144–145.*

made attempts recently; they've gathered in the surrounding area, and the tension is such that they could galvanise forces at any moment."

If that were to happen, Sittwe's once strong Muslim population would be no more. Aung Htay, from the Rakhine Nationalities Development party, which has 35 seats in parliament, said the aggression from Arakanese was needed to retain a hold on the state. "We never wanted to fight the Bengalis," he said, echoing the claim that the term Rohingya is a political construct. "We want to protect our land though, so we must fight."

The result has been the creation of an apartheid-like state, where more than 100,000 Muslims have been driven into camps. They add to the nearly 300,000 Rohingya living stateless in Bangladesh, and countless thousands more in countries such as Malaysia and Thailand. Such is the intensity of the latest campaign that observers are debating whether ethnic cleansing is under way.

Increase in Anti-Muslim Attacks

Attacks from Buddhist mobs in recent weeks have widened to include Kaman Muslims, who are distinct from the Rohingya and have citizenship. Until October they had lived relatively harmoniously with the Buddhist population. Smith says that this factor, coupled with a grenade attack on a mosque in Karen state, eastern Burma, raises the possibility that a religious war is unfolding. "There is a nationwide anti-Muslim sentiment," he said. "What we are seeing in Arakan state is as much about ethnicity as it is about religion."

A two-hour boat ride upriver from Sittwe, the monasteries of Mrauk U have become home to hundreds of Arakanese sheltering from the violence. It was nearby villages such as Yaithein that fell victim to grisly retaliatory attacks from Muslim groups. But restrictions on movement by the authorities, coupled with a climate of fear among Buddhists and Muslims, has impeded investigation of both sides of the violence.

A commission set up by the government to look into the unrest has already met with obstacles. Zarganar, a popular comedian and member of the commission, lamented last month that local leaders from both sides were not co-operating in the investigation.

"Once you take the lid off authoritarian rule, then you will have these sudden outbursts," said fellow commission member Aung Naing Oo, adding, however, that the multifarious channels that have opened with the reforms offer hope for reconciliation. "There is segregation now, but the Myanmar [Burmese] government as far as I know does not have a segregation policy."

An air of hostility hangs over Sittwe. The feeling here is that deep-seated animosities will take years to resolve. Both Arakanese and Rohingya say they have cut all contact with long-time friends from the now rival communities. In downtown Sittwe, shops that had belonged to Muslims have been appropriated by the authorities; their former owners do not risk the journey out of Aung Mingalar to work.

The future of the state hangs in the balance. Past experiences with the Burmese government cast doubt on the official death toll of 180—it may be that the scale of the violence is far greater than outsiders have been led to believe.

"I saw at least 21 bodies before I left," said Khamal Alam of his parting image of Kyaukphyu. He has already lived as a stateless Rohingya in a country growing increasingly hostile to Muslims, and bitterness now pervades both sides. The fear now is that this conflict has gone beyond being merely one over ethnic identity. "I hate Buddhists," he said. "Now I have no family, no business and no home."

Economic Turmoil Fuels Anti-Rohingya Violence

Asma Masood

The author of the following viewpoint explains that the conflict between Muslims and Buddhists in Burma is driven by the competition for resources. A variety of economic and political factors during and after the era of British rule in Burma placed the groups in conflict. The author also explores how natural disasters and the availability of international aid have also played a role in stoking animosity between the two groups. She concludes that economic factors and the spread of aggression among Muslim groups must both be addressed in order to reach a peaceful resolution to conflict in the area. Asma Masood is a research intern with the Centre for Southeast Asia Research Program at the Institute of Peace and Conflict Studies in New Delhi, India.

The Rohingya issue is seen less as a clash between religions and more of an ethnic and economic problem within Myanmar's rapidly developing economy.[1] The TOI [*Times of India*] report also quotes an investment consultant that there is competition for land and resources after the country opened its economy. He adds that the fundamental cause of tension in Rakhine [Arakan] is largely economic.

How have economic factors contributing to conflict in Rakhine state evolved? What impact does international aid have on the conflict? Can the conflict be bracketed as merely economic?

A Storm in Rakhine's Rice Bowl

The Rakhine people have perceived the Rohingya as competitors for land since colonial times. Rakhine peasants who had fled British annexation returned to find their lands were occupied

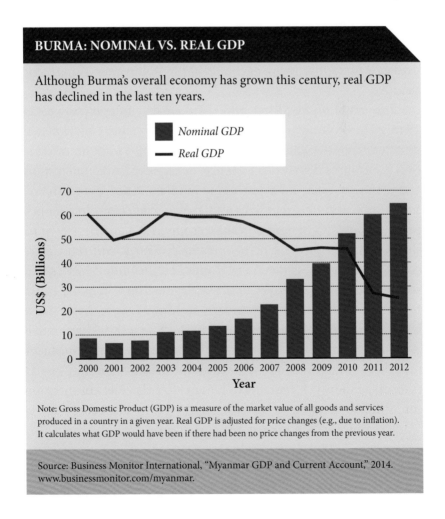

BURMA: NOMINAL VS. REAL GDP

Although Burma's overall economy has grown this century, real GDP has declined in the last ten years.

Note: Gross Domestic Product (GDP) is a measure of the market value of all goods and services produced in a country in a given year. Real GDP is adjusted for price changes (e.g., due to inflation). It calculates what GDP would have been if there had been no price changes from the previous year.

Source: Business Monitor International, "Myanmar GDP and Current Account," 2014. www.businessmonitor.com/myanmar.

by Rohingya rice farmers on a long-term lease basis, rented out by colonizers. The Rohingya also displayed hostility, fearing a threat to their religious identity. Another source of resource conflict in Rakhine (Arakan) state was evident in British accounts from late 19th century: "Bengalis are a frugal race, who can pay without difficulty a tax that would press very heavily on the Arakanese. . . . (They are) not addicted like the Arakanese to gambling, and opium smoking, and their competition is gradually ousting the Arakanese."[2] The competition referred to here may have been for the well-paying administrative and military posts where the British favoured the Rohingya for aiding allied efforts against Japan. However the Rohingya soldiers, when on patrol attacked Rakhine people and villages on their path. These incidents are juxtaposed with accounts of the Rohingya's "hunger for land".[2]

The situation reversed after Myanmar's independence [in 1948]. The Rohingya became stateless and victims of violence directed from the Rakhines. Ethnic conflict also took manifestation in resource deprivation. Hence, decades of land confiscation and arbitrary taxes have left many landless. They found themselves increasingly excluded from their agricultural livelihood. Some struggle as tenants or sharecroppers. Even they have to shell out tax from meager incomes on livestock and other perceived major possessions. Peril to life and livelihood has driven many Rohingya to desert entire villages. The Times of India report states that displacement of Rohingya since Myanmar's transformation was driven to ensure land for factories. The move is to aid the manufacturing sector. There are fears that displacement will cause shortage of farmers and impact the state's agricultural economy. It remains to be seen if the perceived shortage can diminish tensions.

Dynamics of Rakhine state's agricultural economy may also be conflict factors. These include a 2010 state ban on inter-state trade of cultivated rice. It led to a drop in rice prices and lower profits. Consequently the Rakhines will grow more protective

Riots rage in a business district in central Burma in 2013. Economic factors, such as a 2010 state ban on the interstate trade of cultivated rice, fuel violent outbreaks in the country. © AP Photo.

of their product. This may be a factor for them refusing to sell rice to the Rohingya. The level of conflict was to such a level that a Rakhine trader was killed in 2012 for having sold rice to Rohingya.

The situation was exacerbated by forces of nature playing havoc on the economy. Cyclone Giri in 2010 destroyed large tracts of crop fields. Ensuing shortages cause higher restrictions on Rakhine traders' sales to the Rohingya. The storm also led to difficulties for aid agencies to supply rice for displaced Rohingya in camps. It increases their impetus to migration and thus exposure to conflict.

The factors of ethno-economic conflict have caused a spike in international aid to Rakhine state. They desire economic stability to ensure a proper investment climate for crucial projects in the region. This trend is not deemed favourable for decreasing the rhythm of conflict.

The Impact of Aid on the Conflict

Humanitarian agencies voice concern[3] that the high influx of aid can indirectly fuel the Rohingya-Rakhine conflict. The separation of the Rohingya Internally Displaced Persons (IDPs) in aid-funded camps can result in further dividing the two communities in the long term. Moreover the desirable goal of enabling their return is less prioritized. Another issue makes reconciliation more out of reach: Ethnic Rakhines displaced by the conflict are uneasy as the higher amount of aid is directed towards Rohingya IDPs.

A Complex Conflict

The forces of economy and aid have thus shaped the Rakhine conflict to an extent. However the clash cannot be bracketed as merely one based on resources. Evidence is seen in the spreading of aggression and boycotts against other Muslim groups in Myanmar. There are isolated incidents of attacks which spark months of atrocities on each other. The [Buddhist anti-Muslim] 969 Movement is also a case in point. Hence the conflict is clearly a resource-cum-ethnic based issue. Clarity in categorization enables the concerned agencies to approach stemming the concern. Until both root causes are addressed, the chances of resolution are dim.

Notes

1. *Times of India*, 2013. http://articles.timesofindia.indiatimes.com/2013-07-11/rest-of-world/40513721_1_rohingyas-buddhism-buddhists.
2. School of Oriental Studies, 2005, http://www.soas.ac.uk/sbbr/editions/file64388.pdf.
3. http://www.irinnews.org/report/98351/analysis-myanmar-s-rakhine-state-where-aid-can-do-harm.

The Rohingya May Have Links to Islamic Terrorist Groups

Ashis Biswas

In the following viewpoint, a commentator reviews the growing international concern, particularly in South Asia, about the potential links between Rohingya in Burma and radical Islamist organizations. The author writes that there is conflicting information from India and Bangladesh regarding camps for Rohingya in the latter and whether such camps are being used to train insurgent extremists. Population growth among the Rohingya has increased aid from Muslim countries, the author writes. It has also alarmed the Burmese government, which fears that the Rohingya are trying to take over Arakan province to exploit its natural resources. According to the author, India should increase its security operations in the east given the possibility for continued violence and insurgency in the area. Ashis Biswas is an opinion writer for Millennium Post, *an English-language newspaper in New Delhi, India.*

There is a growing international concern about the political linkage between Rohingya Muslims settled in the Rakhine (Arakan) province of Myanmar [Burma] and Islamic fundamentalist organisations. Bangladesh authorities recently rejected official Indian claims about the location of Rohingya camps running close to the Myanmar international border in the Chittagong Hill tracts area, to provide them weapons training. According to Indian Intelligence sources, these camps have been running for the last 6–7 months [first half of 2013]. The objective is to train and arm one section of the persecuted community to defend itself and counter attack, during future outbreaks of ethnic violence in Myanmar.

The matter was discussed at the recent home secretary–level talks between the two countries. However, Bangladesh officials ruled out the existence of any such camps and said they would never allow their territory to be misused by foreign armed groups. Relations between India and Bangladesh over regional security and related matters have been much better with [Bengali political party] Awami League ruling the latter country. India has not yet reacted officially to Bangladesh's views. It may be recalled that even in the recent past, there used to be some disagreement between the two South Asian neighbours regarding the functioning of training camps for hostile armed insurgents. Bangladesh accused India of aiding and harbouring Chakma insurgents during the BNP [Bangladesh National Party] rule. India provided a list of 80 or more camps run by ULFA [United Liberation Front of Assam], NDFB [National Democratic Front of Bodoland] and other insurgents [supported by Bangladesh]. Both countries used to deny, almost routinely, such claims and assured each other nothing would be done to disturb good neighbourly relations.

Ties Between Rohingya and Outside Groups

On one occasion however, the presence of tribal Tripura [India] insurgent organisations in Comilla [Bangladesh] was established when two rival armed groups fought and killed each other on Bangladesh soil, some years ago. Regarding the latest disagreement between India and Bangladesh, regional security experts are yet to express an opinion. However, there is universal agree-

GROWTH OF MUSLIM POPULATION IN THE ASIA-PACIFIC REGION

Estimated Number of Muslims, 1990–2030

Region	1990	Percent Increase 1990–2010	2010	Percent Increase 2010–2030	Projected 2030
Central-Western Asia	167,142,000	43.6%	240,005,000	26.5%	303,691,000
South Asia	317,571,000	59.7%	507,284,000	34.8%	683,793,000
Southeast-East Asia	188,339,000	36.8%	257,715,000	19.2%	307,256,000
The Pacific	226,000	122.7%	503,000	75.9%	885,000

Share of the Population That Is Muslim, 1990–2030

Region	1990	Point Change 1990–2010	2010	Point Change 2010–2030	Projected 2030
Central-Western Asia	89.3%	+ 5.2 pts	94.4%	+ 0.7 pts	95.2%
South Asia	28.1%	+ 3.3	31.4%	+ 2.5	33.9%
Southeast-East Asia	10.6%	+ 1.4	12.0%	+ 1.0	12.9%
The Pacific	0.8%	+ 0.6	1.4%	+ 0.6	2.0%

Population estimates are rounded to thousands. Percentages are calculated from unrounded numbers. Figures may not add exactly due to rounding.

Source: Pew Research Center's Forum on Religion and Public Life, "The Future of the Global Muslim Population," January 2011, p. 72. www.pewforum.org.

ment that a section of Rohingya Muslims maintain close links with international Islamic terror groups and civil rights organisations. Recently, a group of Rohingyas met in Saudi Arabia to discuss the present situation in Myanmar and seek a political solution to the continuing ethnic crisis and strife. Rohingyas also addressed a recent rally organised by the Indonesian Forum Umat Islam organisation in Jakarta [Indonesia] last month,

About thirty-four thousand Rohingya live in the Kutupalong camp in southern Bangladesh, seen here in 2011. The refugees have been accused of having ties with Islamic terrorist groups. © Thierry Falise/LightRocket via Getty Images.

seeking moral and material support, according to media reports. Veteran analyst Bertil Lintner feels that Rohingyas may well have sought international help and recalls that they had often worked closely with the (just banned) Jamate-Islami party in Bangladesh. Myanmar authorities, who continue to suppress the Rohingyas ruthlessly, not recognising them as ethnic Burmese at all, claim that the "foreign Bengali Muslims from Bangladesh" are actually out to establish first an autonomous and then an independent breakaway Arakan province, in view of [the] rich offshore hydrocarbon resources of the region.

Their population has also increased rapidly in recent years, threatening local indigenous communities. There is evidence of Saudi Arabia–based charity groups like Rabita and others helping the community to spread Islam locally. According to the local Burmese view, most Rohingyas are a product of a union between "Bangladeshi fathers and Burmese mothers." The Burmese maintain the Muslims were brought into Burma by the British [who ruled Burma 1824–1948] into their territory and they later settled permanently. At one time, they numbered almost a million. Successive waves of targeted anti-Muslim attacks resulted in the exodus of some 250,000 of them to Bangladesh some years ago and another 150,000 in recent months. At least 200 people were killed in group attacks and clashes, but many more perished while trying to flee by boats, aiming to reach Bangladesh, Thailand, Malaysia, Indonesia or Singapore, through starvation or drowning. Bangladesh no longer accepts Rohingya refugees, nor do the other countries. Only Thailand has allowed some 2,000 or so to settle into temporary camps pending their deportation. A smaller number has been accommodated in Malaysia and Indonesia. Along with Thailand, these countries have urged upon Myanmar to settle the Rohingya issue.

Government Responses to the Potential Threat

So far, there has been no categorical response from Naypitaw [the Burmese capital and government]. Quite apart from ethnic differences, the Islamic terror linkage of the Rohingyas [is what] most countries in the region find disturbing. Indonesia has seen angry anti-Myanmar demonstrations by large crowds, in support of the Rohingyas. India, too, has reasons for concern. A group of nearly 3,000 Rohingyas have turned up in Delhi [the national capital district], to protest outside the office of the UNHCR [United Nations High Commissioner for Refugees]. According [to] media sources, most have been put up in local mosques by their "sympathisers," who are led and organised by the former Vice Chancellor of Jamia Millia University [in Delhi], Nawaz Zafar Jung. They want to be settled in India, although by rights they should be the responsibility of Bangladesh or Myanmar or the United Nations. Some Muslim organisations in India have supported their demand. Smaller bands of stranded Rohingyas, believed to be on their way to Pakistan, have been rounded up from West Bengal. The past record of Rohingyas should also cause Indian policymakers worry. Members of the community have participated in the anti-Soviet operations of Islamic Jehadis in Afghanistan. Some have been trained in armed camps there and elsewhere, along with Taliban and Al Qaeda activists. Presumably these facts make it clear to most governments that if settled in their territory, the Rohingyas could well turn out to be quite a handful, even as a minority.

The Organisation of Islamic [Cooperation] also tried to open an office in Myanmar to help the beleaguered community financially. The Myanmar government did not agree. Given the complexity of the present situation, India can at best wait and watch the situation carefully and step up its own security in the east.

11

The Rohingya Have No Important Links to Islamic Terrorist Groups

Joseph Allchin

In the following viewpoint, originally published by a nonprofit Burmese media organization, the author writes that claims of terrorist activity by the Rohingya are false and overblown. He cites similarities in how the United States and Burma have used myths of external terrorist threats to justify attacks on a perceived enemy. For example, the author accuses the Burmese government of using violence by Rohingya individuals as a pretext for reprisals against the entire ethnic community. He explains that the Rohingya do not pose a credible threat to the sovereignty or wellbeing of Burma. Joseph Allchin is a journalist based in Bangladesh with the Democratic Voice of Burma, the exiled Burmese news network. He has contributed to the Financial Times, The Guardian, *and other publications.*

Ethnic strife is a defining facet of Burmese political life. However, few examples appear so eerily orchestrated as the hounding of the Rohingya, whom the UNHCR [United Nations High Commissioner for Refugees] term "virtually friendless." Much hot air has been expelled to debate the origins of the minority group since communal tensions erupted in late May and early June [2012], but perhaps more telling is the now common refrain that they are "terrorists."

On the 10th of October 2002 the US embassy in Rangoon [Burma] sent a rare cable home to Washington D.C.—rare because it contained intelligence direct from the Burmese military.

It asserted that members of the Arakan Rohingya National Organisation (ARNO) had met with [Al Qaeda terrorist leader] Osama Bin Laden. Further that members of the organisation had sought weapons training in Afghanistan and Libya. The group was then attempting to get bases on the Thai border and join forces with the ethnic armed groups.

"Five members (names still under inquiry by the GOB [Government of Burma]) of ARNO attended a high-ranking officers' course with Al Qaeda representatives on 15 May, 2000."

The Creation of the Bin Laden Myth

On the same day that the cable was sent, across town the US senate approved President George W. Bush's war against Iraq. Both stories were based on a myth—one that was crystallised the previous year in a New York courtroom.

To try Bin Laden in absentia for association with the East Africa embassy bombings of 1998 [in Tanzania and Kenya], the prosecutor in the trial needed evidence of an organised network under the Racketeer Influenced and Corrupt Organisations Act (RICO).

The FBI and the prosecution had one witness who had worked with Bin Laden in the early 90's called Jamal Al Fadl. He "was more than happy" to provide what Jason Burke, author of the seminal work *Al-Qaeda*, told the BBC was the basis of the "first Bin Laden myth"—that there was an organised hierarchical structure in a group called Al Qaeda with Bin Laden at its head.

This was not the case.

Al Fadl had fallen out with Bin Laden after embezzling some $110,000 from him and in return for the key evidence needed to prosecute him under laws used against drug and mafia gangs, the Sudanese militant [was] placed under witness protection and given money from the FBI.

Prior to September the 11th, the term Al Qaeda was not used by Bin Laden. Sam Schmidt, a defence lawyer in the trial of the embassy bombings, said that Al Fadl "lied in a number of specific testimonies" in order to make them, "identifiable as a group and therefore prosecute any person associated with Al Qaeda for any acts or statements made."

ARNO Members Deny Links to Al Qaeda

Named in the 2002 cable is Salim Ullah of the ARNO. Now a resident in Chittagong [Bangladesh], he admits that the group did once maintain arms but renounced armed struggle about a decade ago.

He denies the accusation of Al Qaeda links, calling it pro-paganda and asks, "Karen, Kachin and other people are fighting with the government, they are defending their people, they are fighting for equal rights, so they are freedom fighters, but when we struggle, we are terrorists, is this logical?"

Indeed the US embassy felt they were given the report for a reason, concluding in the 2002 cable that:

> The Burmese view all these [ethnic armed] groups as terrorists. Their purpose in giving us this report is to make sure we are aware of the alleged contacts between ARNO and the Burmese insurgent groups on the Thai border. Presumably, they hope to bolster relations with the United States by getting credit for co-operation on the [Counter-Terrorism] front." ... "Its purpose is probably to draw a connection between Al Qaeda, which has supported ARNO, and Burmese insurgent groups active on the Thai border.

Just like in Bush's ill-fated war in Iraq, where the weapons of mass destruction and links between [Iraqi president] Saddam Hussein and Al Qaeda have yet to be unearthed after almost a decade, no such connections have been made with the Rohingya.

"Have you heard a shot from the Rohingya in the last two decades?" asks Ullah.

But now as the violence rages in Arakan state, with riots and burnings by mobs on both sides, the director of President Thein Sein's office and a graduate of the elite Defence Services Academy, Zaw Htay (aka Hmu Zaw) took to posting his take on the violence in Arakan state on Facebook:

> It is heard that Rohingya Terrorists of the so-called Rohingya Solidarity Organization [formerly a part of the ARNO] are crossing the border and getting into the country with the weapons. That is Rohingyas from other countries are coming into the country. Since our Military has got the news in advance, we will eradicate them until the end! I believe we are already doing it.
>
> We don't want to hear any humanitarian issues or human rights from others. Besides, we neither want to hear any talk of justice nor want anyone to teach us like a saint.

Pretexts for Reprisals

Much like the decision to go to war against Iraq, a sovereign nation with no relation to the attacks on the World Trade Center [on September 11, 2001], the vile act of rape and murder by three individuals was used as an excuse to attack Muslims or those who fit the stereotype with absolutely no connection to the initial crime, which resulted in the June 3rd [2012] massacre of ten non-Rohingya Muslims on a bus returning to Rangoon.

Any claims that it was a direct reprisal is illogical by way of the fact that the rapists had already been detained by that date. Discrimination was thus not an issue of being 'Rohingya' per se, or indeed according to another US Embassy cable even a matter of religion:

> Hindu residents of the state, most of whom are ethnically Indian, suffer the same lack of citizenship rights and restrictions on travel as their Muslims neighbours.

The common denominator being what the state-run *Myanmar Alin* newspaper would designate as being "Kalar"—a pejorative racial slur derived from the Sanskrit word for black or dark.

Warning Shots

Zaw Htay's eradication mission aimed at the Rohingya was reported by Radio Free Asia. Burmese military helicopters, refugees claimed, had been firing on boats of civilians on the Naf River, which divides Burma and Bangladesh, as Rohingyas attempted to cross into the safety of the neighbouring country.

Salim Ullah and others note that Rohingya victims of the rioting have been turning up in hospitals on both sides of the border with bullet wounds, even though the mobs of ethnic vigilantes on both sides have only possessed crude weapons. He asserts that no Arakanese have suffered similar injuries.

Activists have noted that the military has acted in concert with Arakanese vigilantes, although this is hard to confirm, but the argument has strong historical precedent. In both 1978 and 1991 the military committed serious pogroms against the Rohingya, which resulted in hundreds of thousands fleeing their homes.

The US embassy struggled to find evidence of organised violent actions that other ethnic armies have undertaken. In 2003 they noted: "There has been no serious insurgent activity in northern Rakhine State for several years," only finding that:

A French NGO worker related an incident from 2001 in which four members of the security forces were murdered at night in their camp. He believed it had something to do with forced prostitution or trafficking in women and was probably not insurgent related. After the murders, she continued, the security forces rounded up the inhabitants of a nearby village and penned them in a field for two days with no food or water. Two toddlers, who were left at the village, reportedly died.

The murder of the security forces they note was probably "the result of local resentments and outraged husbands or fathers." A similar crime, it must be noted, as the awful murder and rape of Ma Thidar Htwe [a Rakhine].

Myths Used for Political Gain

Like most myths there is a grain of truth that germinates into a political tool. Bin Laden of course was himself a financer of jihad, but he was not the leader of an international, organised hierarchy and especially did not have support from Iraq during the Saddam [Hussein] era.

Similarly, Bangladesh has violent Islamist groups, some of whom have links with groups in other Muslim countries. They have probably utilised the desperation of individual Rohingya, either domestically in Bangladesh or in Pakistan and Afghanistan.

However, there is no evidence of camps or jihadi terrorists in Burma, least of all running around burning down houses.

The ARNO likewise may have received funding and assistance from Islamist groups but the very notion that they were part of a large organised criminal conspiracy is made highly questionable by the lack of terrorist activity. The Karen National Union [the political organization representing the Karen ethnic group in Burma] receives support from churches, despite having had a more active war over their lifetime.

The spinning of the myth in both cases serves grander strategic aims. For the Burmese military the idea of sovereignty and the institution's raison d'etre are intwined.

On Armed Forces Day this year, state TV reported that in 1988 the armed forces prevented the country from falling into "foreign servitude."

The idea that the protests in 1988 were caused by a foreign enemy is of course a fantasy but the notion is to split patriotic sentiment from dissent. [Opposition leader Aung San] Suu Kyi and the 88 protesters by [that] rationale were "foreign stooges."

Now some of those that the military would have labelled "foreign stooges" have in turn joined in rounding on an imagined army of "foreign servitude"—the Rohingya.

Rohingya refugees from Burma headed to Malaysia are rescued at sea by officers of the Thai navy in 2013. © Yongyo Pruksarak/EPA/Newscom.

The [pro-democracy 88 Generation Students] group's Ko Ko Gyi stated that the problems in Arakan state were because of "illegal immigration," and that "they were offending the sovereignty" of the country.

There is nothing to suggest however that the murderous libido of the rapists was influenced by their legal status in the country.

"If the powerful countries forced us to take responsibility for this issue we will not accept it," Ko Ko Gyi said in an interview. "If we are forced to yield we, the army and the democratic [forces] will deal with the issue as a national issue."

Imagined External Enemies

The sense of being threatened by an outside enemy is palpable in his words. This addresses two quarters—the imagined jihadi army and the same concerned international community who supported him and his comrades through decades of military rule (much to the anger of the military government).

It is reminiscent of the decision to move [the country's capital] Naypyidaw to the precise middle of the country where, as the President's chief political adviser Ko Ko Hlaing said, it was as far away as possible from all the imagined threats on the borders.

Ko Ko Gyi's prominent colleague Min Ko Naing, a *nom de guerre* which translates to "Conqueror of Kings," was more measured but with no sense of irony when he said, "it is most important to prevent incitement that would cause riots."

Min Ko Naing was incarcerated precisely for inciting riots in 1988 and 2007.

If 800,000 of the poorest people in a country infringed upon its sovereignty, then the Burmese migrants in Thailand have surely conquered that Kingdom several times over.

In the end there are no winners from this strife apart from the military. By creating a phantom enemy and exploiting long present communal tensions the military has gained vital cross-section support and thereby power.

CHAPTER 3

Personal Narratives

Chapter Exercises

1. **Writing Prompt**

   Imagine that you are a Rohingya teen living in a Burmese ghetto. Write a diary entry where you explain whether you would prefer to be legally integrated into Burmese society or to be relocated to a country that welcomes resettled Rohingya. Give details about your current life and describe all aspects of your life that you hope will be improved by the change to explain the reasons for your preference.

2. **Group Activity**

   Form two groups for a debate. One group will adopt the position that the Rohingya are illegal aliens and should be relocated outside Burma. The other group will argue that the Rohingya should be afforded equal rights as Burmese citizens. Before the debate, study your assigned position as a group and determine what information from viewpoints in this book can be used to support your argument.

Rohingya Survivors Describe Violent Attacks in 2012

Robin McDowell

The author of the following viewpoint relates personal accounts gathered by the Associated Press in northern Rakhine (Arakan) State in Burma in late 2013. According to the author, Rohingya residents of one particular village described the government crackdown that followed a recent spate of ethnic violence in 2012. Residents suffered rape, destruction of personal property, and forced abductions at the hands of security and police forces, according to the viewpoint. The author describes a Burmese judicial system in which trials are far from fair, and torture and squalor are common in the jails. The author further casts doubt on the new civilian government's willingness to make significant change. Robin McDowell is a journalist for the Associated Press, based in Burma.

Noor Jaan lifted her black Islamic veil and recalled the last time she saw her husband. He was among more than 600 Rohingya Muslim men thrown in jail in this remote corner of Myanmar [Burma] during a ruthless security crackdown that followed sectarian violence, and among one in 10 who didn't make it out alive.

Jaan said that when she visited the jail, the cells were crammed with men, hands chained behind their backs, several stripped naked. Many showed signs of torture. Her husband, Mohammad Yasim, was doubled over, vomiting blood, his hip bone shattered.

"We were all crying so loudly the walls of the prison could have collapsed," the 40-year-old widow said.

"They killed him soon after that," she said of her husband. Her account was corroborated by her father, her 10-year-old son and a neighbor. "Other prisoners told us soldiers took his corpse and threw it in the forest."

"We didn't even have a chance to see his body," she said.

The sectarian violence that has gripped this predominantly Buddhist nation of 60 million in the last 16 months [August 2012 through November 2013] has been most intense in the western state of Rakhine, where 200 people have been killed in rioting and another 140,000 forced to flee their homes. Three-quarters of the victims have been Muslims—most of them members of the minority Rohingya community—but it is they who have suffered most at the hands of security forces.

Severe Punishment for the Rohingya

For every Buddhist arrested, jailed and convicted in connection with mob violence across Rakhine state, roughly four Rohingya went to prison, according to data compiled by the Associated Press [AP].

Members of the ethnic minority often have been severely punished, even when there is little or no evidence of wrongdoing. For example, Amnesty International says [community leader] Dr. Tun Aung was summoned by authorities to try to help ease tensions but could not quiet the agitated crowd. He was arrested a week later, labeled an agitator and is serving nine years in prison. The human-rights group calls the doctor a prisoner of conscience.

Nowhere have Rohingya—described by the U.N. as one of the most persecuted religious minorities in the world—been more zealously pursued than in northern Rakhine, which sits along the coast of the Bay of Bengal and is cut off from the rest of the country by a parallel running mountain range.

It's home to 80 percent of Myanmar's 1 million Rohingya. Some descend from families that have been here for generations. Others arrived more recently from neighboring Bangladesh. All have been denied citizenship, rendering them stateless. For decades, they have been unable to travel freely, practice their religion, or work as teachers or doctors. They need special approval to marry and are the only people in the country barred from having more than two children.

A half-century of brutal military rule in Myanmar ended when President Thein Sein's quasi-civilian government took power in 2011. But in northern Rakhine, where Buddhist security forces have been allowed to operate with impunity, many say life has only gotten worse for Rohingya.

Zura Khatun holds a picture of her son Baseer, who was detained for his alleged role in deadly sectarian rioting against Buddhists in 2012 and was killed while in custody. © AP Photo/ Gemunu Amarasinghe.

"As far as I know, not a single member of the security forces has even been questioned," said the U.N. special rapporteur on human rights in Myanmar, Tomás Ojea Quintana, calling on the state to investigate allegations of official brutality.

"This government needs to understand it has a responsibility toward its people, that there has to be some accountability."

Despite more than a half-dozen inquiries by phone and email, presidential spokesman Ye Htut refused to comment about allegations of abuse by soldiers, police and security forces linked to sectarian violence.

The AP in September [2013] became the first foreign media organization to be granted access to northern Rakhine, which has been under a government crackdown since ethnic violence erupted there on June 8, 2012.

Thousands of knife- and stick-wielding Rohingya rioted in the township of Maungdaw, killing 10 Buddhists, including a monk, and torching more than 460 Buddhist homes, according to state advocate general Hla Thein. The violence came in reaction to a deadly Buddhist attack on Muslim pilgrims in southern Rakhine that was sparked by rumors of a gang rape by Muslim men.

Villagers Describe Abuse

Most of the anti-Buddhist bloodshed occurred in Ba Gone Nar, a rambling village of 8,000 and home to Jaan and dozens of others interviewed by the AP.

Made up of dark teak homes on stilts, Ba Gone Nar is divided by a web of dusty foot paths. Residents peered cautiously through the slats of tall bamboo fences, then eagerly beckoned the journalists through their gates. Some pulled out pictures of sons, brothers or fathers who have been imprisoned since their arrests in the weeks that followed the violence.

For months, residents said, soldiers, police and members of a feared border security unit known as Nasaka showed up at homes, hauling in more than 150 men.

Those left behind have held on to whatever evidence they had, no matter how small. Men with tired, weathered faces dragged out plastic buckets filled with broken glasses, dishes, picture frames—belongings wrecked when security forces ransacked their houses.

Villagers said security forces beat them, looted gold and other valuables and raped women.

"As soon as they came inside, we couldn't do anything," said a 64-year-old woman who alleges she and her two daughters were raped by members of Nasaka. Her voice trembling, she asked not to be named, saying she feared reprisals.

"We were afraid. If they wanted to kill, they would," she said, shrouding much of her face with a light blue headscarf so that she could speak on camera. "They did whatever they wanted. Made us feel . . . that we are nothing," she said.

Zura Khatun was among many residents who said security forces arrested relatives who had done nothing wrong. Some said people who were not even in the area at the time of the riots were taken away.

"They came into our house and destroyed everything. They didn't even leave a single plate we were using," said Zura Khatun, 50. "And then . . . they took my 30-year-old son, Baseer."

Noor Mamed, a neighbor, said he saw Baseer's arrest from his home.

"Nasaka, security police and soldiers were dragging Baseer, hitting him with a gun many times, as his mother and wife begged them to stop," the 67-year-old said. "They grabbed both his hands on one side, and his two legs on the other, and threw him onto the truck like trash."

Zura Khatun clutched a picture of Baseer close to her chest while she was interviewed. It was taken shortly after he was detained and shows him squatting on the ground, looking up at the camera with glazed, terrified eyes.

Baseer was taken first to a detention center in Maungdaw. Days later he was taken 25 kilometers (14 miles) away to

Buthidaung, where a larger jail is reserved for more hardened criminals.

"I went to see him," said Zura Khatun, her cheeks moist with tears. "But when I got there, less than two weeks later, they turned me away. They said he was dead."

Chris Lewa, director of Arakan Project, an independent humanitarian-based research group that has spent nearly a decade documenting abuses in the region, said 966 Rohingya from northern Rakhine were jailed after the riots: 611 in northern Rakhine jails, where 62 inmates died (all in Buthidaung), and another 287 at the jail in the state capital, Sittwe, where she tallied another six prisoner deaths.

The numbers were based on testimony from family members and released inmates. Lewa said many inmates were denied life-saving medical treatment for injuries sustained during arrest or from torture and beatings in jail—both by wardens and Buddhist Rakhine inmates.

Quintana said he has gathered statistics on prisoner deaths that are similar to Lewa's. He said jail conditions appeared to have improved by the time he last visited northern Rakhine in August [2013], but he added that there were credible reports that sick, elderly and underage inmates had been temporarily moved to other locations before his visit.

Questionable Judicial Process

Northern Rakhine is the only place in Myanmar where Buddhists were the main targets of mob violence, and the only place in the country where most people are Muslim. Hla Thein said that across Rakhine state, at least 147 Muslims and 58 Buddhists were killed.

Rohingya make up not only the vast majority of victims, but the vast majority of suspects. Data collected from rights groups, courts, police and other officials indicate that at least 1,000 mostly Rohingya Muslims and 260 Buddhists were arrested following the statewide riots.

More than 900 trials have been held in northern Rakhine, all against Rohingya, according to Lewa. Three were sentenced to life in prison in August for the killing of the monk, she said, and many others got up to 17 years behind bars. Those accused of lesser crimes such as arson got between three and 10 years.

Less than a dozen have been acquitted.

Many defendants were tried without the benefit of defense lawyers, Lewa said. There were no translators or family members present. Some were tried collectively, according to Quintana.

"These kinds of proceedings are not following any kind of process of law or judicial guarantees," he said. "In many cases, it's not clear what charges have been filed against each of these prisoners."

One of the only steps the government has taken to address abuses since the sectarian crisis flared has been to disband Nasaka in July, largely over fears the U.S. was preparing to slap it with sanctions.

The announcement won international praise. But Thein Sein's government has made no effort to explain what happened to its former members. Human-rights activists and Rohingya speculate that they were simply transferred to other units.

During the AP's visit to northern Rakhine, one soldier escorting Myanmar dignitaries carried a gun with a Nasaka insignia. And officials said a new security force made up of police and immigration officers, operating out of the old Nasaka camp, has assumed many of the responsibilities that the former, feared border security unit held.

"They are no different than Nasaka. So don't start thinking about freedom." Ba Thun Aung, the Buddhist Rakhine administrator of Ba Gone Nar, told Rohingya villagers, according to his own account.

Ba Thun Aung said that among other things, the new force is tasked with keeping much-hated family lists in which Rohingya are registered or "blacklisted." Children born to unwed parents, or those who have already met a two-child limit imposed only on Rohingya, are not recognized by the government and are not eligible for such basics as public education and health care.

With no ethnic violence in northern Rakhine for more than a year, some Rohingya say security forces aren't as brutal as they once were.

But some, like Jaan, whose husband was killed in jail, have lost hope that the persecution of their people will ever end.

"It's better," she said, "if Allah just takes our lives."

A Rohingya Survivor Describes Persecution and Violence

Hamid and Emma Crichton

"Hamid" is a Rohingya refugee in Bangladesh originally from Arakan State, Burma. The following viewpoint includes the translated text of a letter he wrote to increase awareness of the plight of the Rohingya in Burma. Hamid describes the conditions under which he fled his native land and provides details about the persecution of Rohingya Muslims in Burma. He expresses concern that the international community is not getting accurate information. According to Hamid, people who disseminate reports about the mistreatment of the Rohingya Muslim minority face decades in prison. Emma Crichton, a master's graduate of the Refugee Studies Centre at the University of Oxford, was researching the impact of forced migration for Rohingya refugees and the host Bangladesh population in Cox's Bazar District when she published Hamid's letter in OpenDemocracy.net, a non-profit website that disseminates news and opinion about international politics and culture.

Since June 2012 the Rohingya have been subject to an intense spate of inter-communal violence and state-sanctioned persecution in Myanmar (Burma). Reports of untold deaths, thousands of homes being destroyed, and tens of thousands of Rohingya being displaced have coincided with a time of great change for the country as it transitions to democracy.

The Rohingya are a Muslim minority from Rakhine [Arakan] State in western Burma, and have been acknowledged by the United Nations to be one of the most persecuted minorities in the world. For decades, the estimated 800,000 population from Rakhine State has confronted restrictions on their freedom of movement, marriage, education, and worship. In 1982 the Government of Burma enacted the 'Burma Citizenship Law' constitutionally excluding the Rohingya people from citizenship, making them a stateless people. At the heart of the tension lies a contested history of the origins of the Rohingya. The Burmese government considers them to be illegal immigrants from Bangladesh.

Bangladesh, as the eighth most populated country in the world, is estimated to be host to over 200,000 Rohingya refugees. Whilst many refugees have resided in Bangladesh since 1978, with another key migration in 1991, the recent arrival of those fleeing persecution from Burma has stirred ongoing tensions. Competition over scarce resources and employment is said to have fueled these tensions between local residents and the Rohingya. This, along with the Government of Bangladesh's suspension of humanitarian aid in refugee camps in July 2012, prompted my investigations about the protection needs of the Rohingya.

After making research inquiries into the consequences of forced migration on both the Rohingyas and the local Bangladesh host population in the Cox's Bazar District of southern Bangladesh, I met a community with a resounding plea for international help and for others to know the Rohingya story.

One young man, Hamid, wrote this letter, and requested his testimony be shared.

[Editor's note: Where marked, the text below is [redacted] for Hamid's security. Grammar has been altered for ease of reading. In all other respects this is an unedited translation of Hamid's letter.]

Who I Am

I finished my primary study in U Hla Pae village and continued my high school in Buthidaung Township. After I finished my study, I continued to study politics. However I could not live in my hometown and had to flee to Bangladesh, and am now living in Cox's Bazar. Bangladesh government also arrested me here with illegal entry to Bangladesh from Myanmar. It is very difficult to get a job here as an illegal immigrant. We are neither accepted by the Bangladesh government nor Myanmar government. We cannot go back to Myanmar. We would like to request to the international community to show us a peaceful place. I am here now for 5 months. I came here to save my life and feed myself. Because there are so many Rohingya in Bangladesh, we only get work once a week. We do not know what to do. People coming from Myanmar are now starving. These people get food once a day only. The Bangladesh government also arrests them. These people cannot live in cities so they have to stay in countryside villages. My hope is to get donations from rich countries to feed us. [Sentence excluded for confidentiality]. I am very thankful and grateful that you listen to our news. I cannot give information about us because I cannot get in contact with any NGOs.

Reality Behind the Taunggot Event

A group of 52 Muslim pilgrims from Yangon, former capital of Myanmar travelled to the cities in Rakhine state with the purpose of religious activities. For their activities, they had to stay for 45 days in different cities and travelled to Yangon through Taunggot. Taunggot is a crosslink city between Rakhine state and Yangon division. On the way back to Yangon on 3rd June 2012, a Rakhine mob attacked them in Taunggot highway. The mob was so cruel that the pilgrim group was killed inhumanly. They were beaten in head till their brains came out, and slaughtered. That night, the Rakhine mob openly celebrated their successful killings with music and alcohol in Taunggot with the presence of local authorities.

Reality About the Story in Kyauk Ni Maw (Than Dwe)

In Kyauk Ni Maw, a Rakhine girl was in love with a Kaman Muslim boy since their high school. There was another Rakhine boy who loved this Rakhine girl. The two lovers broke up for some reason. In general, Rakhine girls were not allowed to have affairs with Muslims in Rakhine state. Therefore some Rakhines made a plan to kill that girl for not loving someone of the same race ([the] Rakhine boy) and murdered her inhumanly. After she was murdered, her body was left closer to the Muslim village and accused her former lover, the Muslim boy, as the rapist and murderer and arrested him. However according to initial medical report, she was not raped at all. Together with him, two of his Muslim friends were also arrested with the same accusation. With that news, some Rakhine extremists distributed pamphlets to instigate the anger and hatred against Muslims among the Rakhine community.

Reality Behind the Events at Myauk-O, Kyauk Phyu and Kyauk Taw

In Myauk-O, the number of Rakhine villages is more than Muslim villages. Therefore Muslim population is much less than Rakhine population. Rakhine used their numbers as an advantage and killed Muslims above 4,000 by using long knife and guns. Among the victims, 2,500 were children and new born babies. Rakhines attached the new born babies at the edge of steel rods and put into fire. Many Muslim houses were also burnt down. Similar stories in Kyauk Phyu and Kyauk Taw as well.

Reality Behind Sittwe's Crisis

In Sittwe, it started on 7 June 2012. The Rakhine started killing Muslims, burning the houses in Zalla Fara (a Muslim village) and all villagers were killed on that day. It continued to other Muslim villages such as Nazir Fara, Amala Fara, Hausha Fara, San Taw Laik, Bomu Rwar and Bo Pwa Fara with the combination of Rakhines, Police forces, NaSaKa (Burmese Border Security Forces), Lone Tein [riot police] and Military forces. Rakhines used long knives and homemade guns while the government forces [used] guns to kill Muslims.

Muslims were burnt alive in their own houses and some were tied up while being burnt. Children and newborn babies were thrown into the river when the Rakhines got tired of stabbing with knives. Some of the children were also thrown into fire. All the government bodies in Sittwe were involved in helping the Rakhine mob to target Muslims. Rakhines had guns and together with Nasaka, Police and Lone Tein, they directly shot at Muslims. Those who were not killed and became homeless are in refugee concentration camps now.

Muslims from Sittwe tried to flee from their birth places to save their lives and travelled by five small boats to Bangladesh. However those five boats were not accepted by the Bangladesh government and were pushed back towards Burma. Among 5 boats, 3 boats were destroyed by NaSaKa with guns in the sea. The other 2 were also not lucky. There were few pregnant women in those 2 boats and they all died while trying to deliver the baby on the boat. The remaining Muslims were also shot dead by local security forces when they reached back to Rakhine state side.

Local security forces were famous for torturing and raping Muslim women previously. In this crisis, they did not stay behind doing all those atrocities towards Muslim girls. The government never take action for that. The monks also encouraged and instigated the Rakhines to kill Muslims. Moreover, the monks were involved by themself to kill and drive away Muslims from their land by changing their clothes to ordinary people.

Reality Behind Maungdaw's Crisis

In Maungdaw, it was started on 8 June 2012. When the problem started in Maungdaw between Rakhine and Muslims, NaSaKa supported to first Rakhines to kill Muslims. When there was a big chance of a riot starting in Maungdaw, a Rakhine trashed a

Lack of drinking water, malnutrition, and threats of violence are serious problems for the thousands of Rohingya refugees in the Kutupalong camp in Bangladesh, shown here in 2009. © Majority World/UIG via Getty Images.

Muslim with his motor bike on 8 June 2012 at 12 PM. After hitting the Muslim, he ran away and the police came and arrested and tortured the victim instead of the Rakhine in the street where the intentional accident happened. When the Muslims (around 10) gathered to the event and asked the police why he was torturing and beating him instead of the Rakhine, the police left the scene with anger and the Muslim was escaped.

That day was Friday and therefore all Muslims go to mosque to pray Juamma at noon. During that time, the police and Na-SaKa force arrived and waited outside till people came out from mosque and shot at Muslims and 2 Muslims died on the spot. When the police and NaSaKa fired shots into the group, people were dispersed and ran away in different directions. After that scene, the Rakhine went to a local mosque and fired it to burn it down. Muslim houses were also burnt down. As the officers shot fire into Muslims, some of them were seriously injured and some of them escaped to Bangladesh to save their life and to treat their injuries. Some are still in Chittagong continuing their treatment and some were dead with their injuries. Back in Maungdaw, Na-SaKa threw some Muslim corpses into the river.

Reality Behind Buthidaung's Crisis

In Buthidaung, there were no clashes yet between Rakhines and Muslims as the Rakhines are the minority there. The military station Sa Kha Ka group no. 15 and Strategy group no. 18 are trying to not have any clashes till today. However the commissioner from the police station commanded the police officers to arrest the educated Muslims from every village and kept them in police custody for 2 days and sent to jail. Some of the Muslims were tortured to death. The police are still arresting the known and rich Muslims and extorting money from them to release them from jails. If the demanded money cannot be provided, the Muslims were tortured inhumanely.

Recently the monks from Buthidaung called a meeting for Rakhines and made a secret plan to bring the guns from Sittwe together with Rakhines from there and stored in Buthidaung. The Muslims are afraid of the guns as they do not have anything to protect themselves. The local government also support the Rakhines and encourage them to attack and oppress Muslims. All of the police are Rakhines and therefore they do not show any mercy to shoot at Muslims. On 3 November 2012, the military seized 180 handmade guns from Rakhines in Buthidaung.

Law and Order in Rakhine State

In 1950s and 1960s, Muslims from Rakhine state from various cities entered to government posts after they finished their study. However now Muslims cannot enter to government jobs at all. Moreover they created different law and order for Muslims in the whole of Rakhine state. Muslims have to follow the rule strictly. No Rakhine has to follow that rule. Muslims cannot marry according to Islamic law. Muslims can only marry after paying 300,000 kyats to NaSaKa (Border security forces). Only Muslims who have money can marry and poor Muslims cannot. If anyone marries without getting permission from NaSaKa they can be sentenced to 5 years according to strict law. Rakhine people do not have such kind of rule. If Muslims have to visit to Maungdaw and Buthidaung, they have to get permission (called Form 4) from the authority. To obtain that form, 5,000 kyats need to be paid and anyone who is caught travelling without that form, he/she will be sentenced to 4 years.

Moreover one cannot live in another house even in the same village without permission. Muslims cannot stay in their relatives' house without any permission from the authority. Otherwise they will be fined 300,000 kyats. It is a very miserable life for Muslims in Rakhine state.

Four years ago, the police forces and NaSaKa forces went to villages in Buthidaung and Maungdaw and gathered all the young girls, young boys and women in police headquarters. They were raped, tortured and beaten inhumanely. Muslims are facing all difficulties to survive in Rakhine state.

Another important matter is that the authority is giving trouble with improper law to UNHCR [United Nations High Commissioner for Refugees] and UNDP [United Nations Development Fund], with the accusation of sending the news of Rakhine state overseas, and sentenced to jails some staff. Those who sent information through the internet and mobile phone are sentenced to 45 years. Therefore some of the real news from Maungdaw and Buthidaung was not sent through internet and phone. Moreover the internet lines were filtered and closed not to be able to send the news. Therefore the international community do not get the real information of Rakhine state. Therefore I am trying now to send the news to international communities.

I hope this letter will reach everyone and after reading this, please help and sympathize to Muslims in Rakhine state.

[Editor's note: This letter is directly translated from the original Burmese letter. Translated by Mohammed Anwar, the current president of the Burmese Rohingya Community in Australia.]

A Rohingya Survivor Describes a Terror Attack

Rohingya Vision

The following viewpoint includes the translated transcript of a radio interview with a Rohingya survivor of a 2012 attack on Kyauktaw, Burma. The interviewee describes being part of a group traveling to Bangladesh and being shot at, robbed, beaten, and tortured by a group of Rakhine (Arakanese) terrorists. According to the survivor, only eleven people out of about 140 survived the attack. Rohingya Vision is a website devoted to reporting on Rohingya issues and news.

Sunday, April 13, 2014—We have earlier [April 10, 2014] reported you that there are as many as 78 Rohingyas from Kyauktaw township missing as armed Rakhine (Maghs) terrorists attacked them in a forest on their way to Buthidaung and Maungdaw. [Note: All locations are in Rakhine State in westernmost Burma]. A bit different to what we have reported earlier, there are 11 people that managed to come back alive from the attack, not 12 (people).

And listen to the interview with a Rohingya survivor of the terror attack. He is from the village of Zailla Fara (Kyauktaw Paikthay) and 24 years old. English translation of the interview is provided. (Interview translated into English by M.S. Anwar.)

Assalamualaikum! (Peace be upon you!)

My name is Mohammed Hashim. I am one of the 11 surviving victims of the terror attack.

We set off for Bangladesh on 7th (April 2014). After we had left (Kyauktaw), we walked for 4:30 hours. Had we walked for half an hour more, we would have reached Aaga Taung (Aaga Mountain).

After that, we encountered with a gang of half-masked Magh (Rakhine) terrorists. Each of them had a gun and a sword. At that time, our (human trafficking) agents were before in front of us and I was behind them. When they shot at us, people began running to and fro and lost contacts with one another. The agents ran away to one direction and I did to another direction.

As I was running, I encountered with other members of the gang. They were about to SLAUGHTER a Rohingya woman.

We became seven people at the place as others, too, were running to their sights like me.

So, the terrorists looted all of our money and belongings. They brutally beat us. They tortured us. Then, they forced us to sit there.

After that, there was sound of gun-shot from Aaga Taung [forest] was heard. They ordered us to sit tight there and not to move away.

Then, they moved towards the Aaga Taung. And they didn't come back. So, we sat tight there until dawn and then, we left the place for a safer place lest we should be caught by other gangs of terrorists.

Then, when we hiked to the top of the mountain, we met with other three people, and one child. So, total four. So, including the agents, there were 11 people in total.

So, we only 11 managed to come alive. We lost contact with other people. Till date, we don't know their whereabouts.

We left from here (Kyauktaw) at 9:30 PM on 7th April 2014. We encountered with the terrorists and they fired at us at 12:30 AM of the night. After that, we lost contact with one another. Those that managed to come back were only 11 including the agents. And we have information of other people. We don't know where they are yet.

They inhumanly beat and tortured us. They inhumanly beat us. We don't know if they were Myanmar military or Rakhine militants. Every one of them had a gun and a sword. They were about 15 people. All of them fired warning shots simultaneously but not at us first. They tied all of us with rope.

When they were about to slaughter us, there was a sound of gun-shot heard from Aaga Taung. So, they left for Aaga Taung and ordered us to sit tight at the place.

We don't know whom the terrorists encountered with after that. They didn't return. It was about dawn. Being worried of other possible attacks, we hiked to top of the Aaga Taung. When we hiked to the top of the mountain, we met with one (Rohingya) person first. Then, one child and in total, we, 11 people, managed to come back.

[Interviewer:] How many were you in total in the group?

[Hashim:] About 130 people!!! Of them, we, only 11 people, came back.

How many men and how many women?

There would be more than 40 women.

How many children?

Children will be around 20. They were going with their mother.

And the rest were adult males?

Of 130 people, there were 40 women, 20 children and the rest were adult males.

Organizations to Contact

The editors have compiled the following list of organizations concerned with the issues debated in this book. The descriptions are derived from materials provided by the organizations. All have publications or information available for interested readers. The list was compiled on the date of publication of the present volume; the information provided here may change. Be aware that many organizations take several weeks or longer to respond to inquiries, so allow as much time as possible.

Amnesty International
5 Penn Plaza, 14th Floor
New York, NY 10001
(212) 807-8400 • fax: (212) 463-9193
e-mail: aimember@aiusa.org
website: www.amnestyusa.org

Amnesty International is a global human rights organization that seeks to promote and protect the basic rights of all individuals worldwide. It envisions a world in which every person enjoys all of the human rights enshrined in the Universal Declaration of Human Rights and other international human rights standards. It publishes reports on its advocacy work and areas of concern throughout the world. Amnesty International's website includes reports and news items, including a section on human rights in Burma.

Arakan Rohingya National Organisation (ARNO)
24 Warwick Road
London, United Kingdom E12 6QP
+44 7947854652
website: http://rohingya.org/portal

ARNO is one of the representative organizations of the Rohingya people of Arakan State, Burma and one of the founding members of the Arakan Rohingya Union. ARNO is devoted to increasing awareness about the Rohingya and ending persecution against them. The London-based organization's website includes news items, reports, videos, and links to other Internet sites about the Rohingya.

Arakan Rohingya Union (ARU)
website: http://ar-union.org

The ARU is an umbrella group for Rohingya organizations from around the world that works to protect the rights of Rohingya Muslims in Burma. It was formed in 2011 at a meeting convened by the Organization of Islamic Cooperation in Jeddah, Saudi Arabia. The organization's website includes a news section, a blog, videos, and photos about the plight of the Rohingya in Burma.

Genocide Watch
PO Box 809
Washington, DC 20044
(202) 643-1405
e-mail: communications@genocidewatch.org
www.genocidewatch.org

Genocide Watch aims to "predict, prevent, stop, and punish genocide and other forms of mass murder" by raising awareness of the eight-stage process of genocide and influencing international policy to curtail potential and actual acts of genocide. Its website includes news alerts and annual reports on countries at risk due to a growing likelihood of genocide or other atrocities. The website also offers links to reports issued by other members of the International Alliance to End Genocide, an international coalition of similar organizations coordinated through Genocide Watch.

Human Rights Watch
350 Fifth Ave., 34th Floor
New York, NY 10118-3299
(212) 290-4700 • fax: (212) 736-1300
e-mail: hrwnyc@hrw.org
website: www.hrw.org

Founded in 1978, this nongovernmental organization conducts systematic investigations of human rights abuses around the world and actively advocates for human dignity. It publishes many books and reports on specific countries and issues as well as annual reports and other articles. Its website includes numerous discussions of human rights and international justice issues, including a special section on Burma.

Institute for the Study of Genocide (ISG)
John Jay College of Criminal Justice
899 Tenth Ave., Room 325
New York, NY 10019
e-mail: info@instituteforthestudyofgenocide.org
website: http://studyofgenocide.org

The ISG is an independent nonprofit organization established in 1982 that promotes and disseminates scholarship and policy analyses on the causes, consequences, and prevention of genocide. It publishes a semiannual newsletter and holds periodic conferences; maintains liaison with academic, human rights, and refugee organizations; provides consultation to representatives of media, governmental, and nongovernmental organizations; and advocates passage of legislation and administrative measures related to genocide and gross violations of human rights.

Montreal Institute for Genocide and Human Rights Studies
Concordia University
1455 De Maisonneuve Blvd.
West Montreal, Quebec H3G 1M8, Canada

(514) 848-2424, ext. 5729 or 2404 • fax: (514) 848-4538
website: http://migs.concordia.ca

Founded in 1986, the Montreal Institute for Genocide and Human Rights Studies (MIGS) monitors native-language media for early warning signs of genocide in countries deemed to be at risk of mass atrocities and collects and disseminates research on the historical origins of mass killings. The institute houses the Will to Intervene Project, a research initiative focused on the prevention of genocide and other mass atrocities. The institute's website provides numerous links to information on genocide and related issues, as well as specialized sites organized by nation, region, or case.

Prevent Genocide International (PGI)
1804 S Street, NW
Washington, DC 20009
(202) 483-1948 • fax: (202) 328-0627
e-mail: info@preventgenocide.org
website: www.preventgenocide.org

PGI is a global education and action network established in 1998 with the purpose of bringing about the elimination of genocide. In an effort to promote education on genocide, PGI maintains a multilingual website for the education of the international community. The website maintains a database of government documents and news releases as well as original content provided by members.

US Department of State
2201 C Street, NW
Washington, DC 20520
(202) 647-4000
website: www.state.gov

The US Department of State is the agency of the federal government responsible for foreign affairs. The website includes daily press briefings, reports on policy issues, and numerous other articles. The office of the historian includes historical information and fact sheets on Burma.

Women's League of Burma (WLB)
website: http://womenofburma.org

The WLB works for the advancement of the status of women towards a peaceful and just society in Burma. In keeping with its mission of eradicating violence and creating a democratic Burma, the WLB conducts programs in peace and reconciliation; political empowerment; women against violence; and advocacy. Its website includes information about its member organizations and provides access to a number of its publications and reports.

World Without Genocide
William Mitchell College of Law
875 Summit Ave.
St. Paul, MN 55105
(651) 695-7621
e-mail: info@worldwithoutgenocide.org
website: http://worldwithoutgenocide.org

World Without Genocide works to protect innocent people around the world. It aims to fight racism and prejudice, advocate for the prosecution of perpetrators, and remember those whose lives and cultures have been destroyed by violence. Its website includes links to resources and discussions of numerous genocides and conflicts, including reports on Burma.

List of Primary Source Documents

The editors have compiled the following list of documents that either broadly address genocide and persecution or more narrowly focus on the topic of this volume. The full text of these documents is available from multiple sources in print and online.

Burma Citizenship Law, October 15, 1982

A Burmese law recognizes 135 official indigenous races and describes a stratified citizenship system based on ancestry. Under the law, citizens are required to obtain a national registration card and noncitizens a foreign registration card.

Convention Against Torture and Other Cruel, Inhuman, or Degrading Treatment or Punishment, United Nations, 1974

A draft resolution adopted by the UN General Assembly in 1974 opposing any nation's use of torture, unusually harsh punishment, and unfair imprisonment.

Convention on the Prevention and Punishment of the Crime of Genocide, December 9, 1948

A resolution of the UN General Assembly that defines genocide in legal terms and advises participating countries to prevent and punish actions of genocide in war and peacetime.

Nobel Lecture by Aung San Suu Kyi, June 16, 2012

Burmese opposition leader and activist Aung San Suu Kyi was awarded the Nobel Peace Prize in 1991, when she was under house arrest. Twenty-one years later, she finally delivered her acceptance speech in Oslo, Norway, saying that the prize meant that "the oppressed and the isolated in Burma were also a part of the world" and "were not going to be forgotten."

Principles of International Law Recognized in the Charter of the Nuremberg Tribunal, UN International Law Commission, 1950

After World War II (1939–1945), the victorious allies legally tried surviving leaders of Nazi Germany in the German city of Nuremberg. The proceedings established standards for international law that were affirmed by the United Nations and later court tests. Among other standards, national leaders can be held responsible for crimes against humanity, which might include "murder, extermination, deportation, enslavement, and other inhuman acts."

Requirements for Bengalis Who Apply for Permission to Marry, Rakhine State Regional Order, May 1, 2005

This policy codifies restrictions on marriage and private relationships imposed against Rohingya by the local authorities. The legal order refers to them as "Bengali" and lists ten requirements for authorities to approve a Rohingya marriage. The process conflicts with certain religious practices and is described by Rohingya as being humiliating and abusive.

Rome Statute of the International Criminal Court, July 17, 1998

The treaty that established the International Criminal Court. It establishes the court's functions, jurisdiction, and structure.

UN General Assembly Resolution 96 on the Crime of Genocide, December 11, 1946

A resolution of the UN General Assembly that affirms genocide is a crime under international law.

Universal Declaration of Human Rights, United Nations, 1948

Soon after its founding, the United Nations approved this general statement of individual rights it hoped would apply to citizens of all nations.

Whitaker Report on Genocide, 1985

This report addresses the question of the prevention and punishment of the crime of genocide. It calls for the establishment of an international criminal court and a system of universal jurisdiction to ensure that genocide is punished.

For Further Research

Books

Imtiaz Ahmed, *The Plight of the Stateless Rohingyas*. Dhaka, Bangladesh: University Press, 2010.

Michael Aung-Thwin and Maitrii Aung-Thwin, *A History of Myanmar Since Ancient Times: Traditions and Transformations*. London: Reaktion, 2012.

Wen-Chin Chang and Eric Tagliacozzo, eds., *Burmese Lives: Ordinary Life Stories Under the Burmese Regime*. New York: Oxford University Press, 2014.

Mikael Gravers, *Nationalism as Political Paranoia in Burma: An Essay on the Historical Practice of Power*, second edition. London: Routledge, 2013.

Michael Jerryson and Mark Juergensmeyer, eds., *Buddhist Warfare*. New York: Oxford University Press, 2009.

Lynn Kuok, *Promoting Peace in Myanmar: US Interests and Role*. Washington, DC: Center for Strategic and International Studies, 2014.

Peter Popham, *The Lady and the Peacock: The Life of Aung San Suu Kyi*. New York: Workman, 2013.

Benedict Rogers, *Burma: A Nation at the Crossroads*. London: Random House, 2013.

David Steinberg, *Burma/Myanmar: What Everyone Needs to Know*. New York: Oxford University Press, 2013.

Nasir Uddin, *Life in Locker: The State of the Rohingyas in Bangladesh*. Saarbrücken, Germany: Scholar's Press, 2013.

Periodicals

BBC, "Burma Census Bans People Registering as Rohingya," March 30, 2014. www.bbc.com.

Charlie Campbell, "Thai Officials Collude in Trafficking of Rohingya Refugees," *Time*, January 7, 2014. http://world.time .com.

Larry Diamond, "The Specter of Mass Killings in Burma," *The Atlantic*, January 31, 2014. www.theatlantic.com.

The Economist, "Ethnic Cleansing in Myanmar: A Bloody Road to Apartheid," October 28, 2012. www.economist.com.

Jonathan Head, "The Unending Plight of Burma's Unwanted Rohingyas," BBC, June 30, 2013. www.bbc.com.

Esther Hitusan, "Lack of Health Care Deadly for Myanmar's Rohingya," Associated Press, May 2, 2014. http://bigstory .ap.org.

Hanna Hindstrom, "The Freedom to Hate," *Foreign Policy*, June 14, 2012. www.foreignpolicy.com.

Joshua Kurlantzick, "Under Fire: The Savage Persecution of Myanmar's Muslim Rohingya," Council on Foreign Relations, December 8, 2012. www.cfr.org.

Fiona MacGregor, "Burma's 'Bin Laden of Buddhism'" *The Telegraph* (UK), July 13, 2013. www.telegraph.co.uk.

Jason Motlagh, "Rohingya Muslims Flee Burma by Boat After Sectarian Violence," *Washington Post*, February 11, 2013. www.washingtonpost.com.

Jane Perlez, "Death Stalks Muslims as Myanmar Cuts Off Aid," *New York Times*, May 2, 2014. www.nytimes.com.

Radio Free Asia, "Citizenship Only for Myanmar's 'Legal' Rohingyas," July 12, 2013. www.rfa.org.

Moshanda Sultana Ritu, "Ethnic Cleansing in Myanmar," *New York Times*, July 12, 2012. www.nytimes.com.

William Saletan, "The Slaughter of Muslims," *Slate*, February 13, 2014. www.slate.com.

Joseph J. Schatz, "Burma's Aung San Suu Kyi, a Human Rights Icon, Is Criticized on Anti-Muslim Violence," *Washington Post*, December 23, 2013. www.washingtonpost.com.

Jake Scobey-Thai, "The Bin Laden of Buddhism and the Axis of Hate," *Sydney Morning Herald*, March 11, 2014. www.smh .com.au.

Habib Siddiqui, "A History of Injustice Ignored: Rohingya: The Forgotten People of Our Time," *American Muslim*, November 20, 2005. http://theamericanmuslim.org.

Brian Tashman, "Geller: Oppose Resolution Condemning Ethnic Cleansing in Burma," Right Wing Watch, December 4, 2013. www.rightwingwatch.org.

Francis Wade, "The Monks Who Hate Muslims," *Foreign Policy*, April 22, 2013. www.foreignpolicy.com.

Graeme Wood, "A Countryside of Concentration Camps," *New Republic*, January 21, 2014. www.newrepublic.com.

Other Sources

Exiled to Nowhere (www.exiledtonowhere.com). Associated with Greg Constantine's photography book of the same name, this website includes information about the Rohingyas' history and plight as well as numerous photographs.

They Call It Myanmar: Lifting the Curtain (Directed by Robert H. Lieberman, PhotoSynthesis Productions, 2012). This documentary was shot secretly in Myanmar and documents life under the military dictatorship. It includes dozens of interviews with Burmese people, including Aung San Suu Kyi, who had been recently released from prison when the documentary was filmed.

Index

Khine Thurein, 60
Ko Aye, 109
Ko Ko Gyi, 131–132
Ko Ko Hlaing, 132
Kuok, Lynn, 94
Kuwait, 95
Kyauk Ni Maw, Myanmar, events,
 146
Kyauk Phyu, Myanmar, events, 146
Kyauk Taw, Myanmar, events, 146
Kyaw Hla Aung, 90
Kyaw San Wai, 92–97

L
Laos, 44
Lebanon, 8
Lemkin, Raphael, 5
Lewa, Chris, 109, 140, 141
Libya, 126
Lintner, Bertil, 122
London School of Economics, 54

M
Ma Thidar Htwe, 130
Magnier, Mark, 56–61
Malaysia, 45, 49, 104, 112, 123
Mann Maung Maung Nyan, 58
Marriage restrictions, 36, 144, 161
Masood, Asma, 114–118
Mass atrocities/killings, 8, 11–13,
 28
 See also Genocide; Rohingya,
  genocide
Maung Zarni, 54
Maungdaw crisis, 147–149, 150,
 152
McDowell, Robin, 135–142
McKinsey, Kitty, 45, 46
Memorandum of Understanding,
 41
Min Ko Naing, 132
Muslim Rohingya
 arrests of, 140–141

Buddhist attack of, 58, 85
Buddhist tensions, 109–110
destruction of homes, *79*
population growth, 121*t*
refugees, 34–35
religious persecution against, 38
 See also Rohingya
Myanmar (Burma)
democratic transformation,
 77–80
ethnic groups in, *31*
freedom from fear, 75–76
freedom from want, 71–72
freedom of expression, 68–71
freedom of worship, 73–75
freedom reforms, 67–68
Islamic radicalization potential,
 95–96, *96*
military rule in, 50–51
overview, 66–67
refugee crisis in, 43–44
US relations with, 94
US support for, 66–76
 See also Aung San Suu Kyi
Myauk-O event, 146

N
"Naga Min" (Operation Dragon
 King), 27
NaSaKa (border security forces)
 disbanding of, 141
 marriage restrictions, 36
 violence by, 138–139, 147–148,
  150
National Democratic Front of
 Bodoland (NDFB), 120
National Democratic Party for
 Development, 61
National League for Democracy
 (NLD), 51–54, 67
National Unity Party, 37
Ne Win (General), 27–28, 82